"*These Fragments I Have Shored* is a brave-beyond-brave memoir for its groundswell of heartache, the surge of brutality and wonder in living in a body that turns on you, the adventures of a true believer in staying alive through the swells of thrash and miracle. A love story to a mother who danced to Elvis, spoke the hard truths, and never gave up—Jason Irwin's writing is inspired, funny, and stunningly honest, an outpouring to the heroes and the monsters in all of us."

—Jan Beatty, *American Bastard*

"Jason Irwin's voice is vital, human, and empathetic, having crafted an engaging memoir that breathes life and urgency into an often moribund genre. Serious, but never dreary, intense but often funny, Irwin's reflections on the trials and trauma of life are never preachy. I've long known Irwin as a poet of immaculate power, with *These Fragments I Have Shored* he further proves my belief that it's poets who make the best writers of prose."

—Ed Simon, *Heaven, Hell and Paradise Lost*

"Jason Irwin's expertly observed, deeply introspective, inspirational memoir has the complex characterization and suspense of a novel. The book's dual timelines of Irwin's caring for his terminally ill mother and of his lifelong struggle with birth defects reveal him as fully as any memoir I've read reveals its narrator. With absolute control and bracing honesty, he works to come to terms with his complicated feelings about his mother's sacrifices for him and his responsibility to take care of her as she loses control of her life and then reality. The book is also about the people, events, and adventurous, resilient spirit that shaped Irwin as a prize-winning, working-class poet. *These Fragments*

I Have Shored is powerful, wise, and vulnerable. You'll thank yourself for reading it."

—Tim Parrish, *Fear and What Follows*

"This is a unique and moving memoir composed in the form of a mosaic, because our memory is made up of intertwined events that are never chronological. The main character reminds me of Marcel Proust, because of his specific, close relationship with his mother. 'Life is full of little tragedies that happen every day,' he says. I recommend this book."

—Wioletta Grzegorzewska, *Swallowing Mercury*

These Fragments I Have Shored

A Memoir

These Fragments I Have Shored

A Memoir

Jason Irwin

Some names and identifying details have been changed to protect privacy.

First Edition

Library of Congress Control Number: 2025948875

Casebound ISBN: 978-1-62720-638-9
Paperback ISBN: 978-1-62720-639-6
Ebook ISBN: 978-1-62720-640-2

Cover Design by Amiyah Cobb

Internal Design by Amiyah Cobb & Cecelia Durborow
Editorial Development by Abby Hill & Samantha Vitale
Promotional Development by Thomas Webb

Published by Apprentice House Press

Loyola University Maryland
4501 N. Charles Street, Baltimore, MD 21210
410.617.5265
www.ApprenticeHouse.com
info@ApprenticeHouse.com

It would be difficult to persuade me that the story of the Prodigal Son is not the legend of a man who didn't want to be loved. When he was a child, everyone in the house loved him. He grew up not knowing it could be any other way and got used to their tenderness, when he was a child.

—Rainer Maria Rilke, *The Notebooks of Malte Laurids Brigge*

Memory conforms to what we think we remember.

—Joan Didion, *Blue Nights*

Get This Body Out of Here

Friday, January 25, 2019

"Jay! Jay!" my mother howled from the back bedroom. I woke and ran in to find her coiled in a fetal position at the foot of her bed.

"You better get this body out of here," she commanded. "I died an hour ago."

I was about to reach out to her, to brush her hair away from her face, and try to calm her. Instead, I pulled back and stood staring at what she'd become. Purple veins, like dried-up tributaries, spread across the sallow topography of her chest. The twin peaks of her clavicle threatened to puncture her skin with each labored breath. Her dark doe eyes held me in their watery gaze, boring into me, feral and pleading.

"What are you talking about?" I snapped. "You're not dead!" Instantly, I realized how bothered I sounded, how annoyed. My mother was dying and all I cared about was getting enough sleep.

*

Six months earlier, before we had any inkling my mother was ill, my partner Jenny and I made the three-hour trip from Pittsburgh to Dunkirk, New York, to spend the weekend with her. It was the height of summer, a couple of weeks before my forty-seventh birthday. My mother felt good, so we decided to go for a drive. The air smelled of fresh cut grass, wildflowers, and diesel. Vineyards rose and fell to our right, while on the left, the cement gray waters of Lake Erie passed in and out of view like the back of a whale. My mother rolled down her window and let the wind sweep across her face while Bob Dylan crooned from the CD player: *Someday baby you ain't gonna worry po' me anymore.*

We drove through Silver Creek and the Seneca reservation to Athol Springs, where we sat outside on a restaurant patio overlooking the lake—the Buffalo and Lackawanna skylines shining in the distance. A flock of white windmills stood on the shore where, when I was a child, the mills of Bethlehem Steel towered and spewed dark plumes of smoke and grime.

Jenny and my mother ordered porterhouse steak with mashed potatoes, while I had walleye, coleslaw, and fries. My mother and I posed for a photograph, our shoulders leaning into one another, our smiles wide.

*

Two years before that summer day, my mother suffered a stroke. We had the habit of talking on the phone at least three times a day. Sometimes more. I called her during my lunch break and as I walked to the bus stop after work. She called to tell me what was happening in Dunkirk, what she'd heard on the news, or to remind me it was my turn at Scrabble, which we played on Facebook. Yet she waited two days before mentioning that she might have had a stroke.

It was a Friday in May. I called several times, but she didn't answer. The day before she sounded groggy, a bit confused. She told me she had a terrible headache and was going to lie down. "You can call me later," she said, "but I might not answer."

When my mother did answer, about 3:30 p.m. the following afternoon, her voice slurred.

"I think I had a stroke," she said.

"Last night?"

"No, Wednesday."

I hung up and called the Dunkirk Police. That night I drove to Erie, Pennsylvania, where she had been taken by ambulance to Hamot Hospital. My mother had suffered an ischemic stroke, due to a buildup of plaque in her carotid arteries.

Even though she hadn't received immediate care, care that may well have prevented her from losing the use of her left arm, my mother was lucky. Her mind wasn't affected. She remained sharp and quick-witted as ever. Even her sarcasm was intact. Doctors put a stent in one of her arteries and released her after a few days. They suggested she go to a rehab facility, but my mother refused. She was adamant about going home to her apartment. With the help of a walker, a home health aide, and an unyielding determination, she managed to live on her own for a few more years, hiding behind a facade of independence and fearlessness.

*

Now, my mother was truly dying, and all I could do was watch her die. She had moved in with us three weeks earlier, leaving her beloved apartment and the town she grew up in behind. That summer day along the lake seemed like a lifetime ago.

As I stood over her bed, the sky outside the window transformed from black to a dull chrome. I watched my mother watching me, then tried to turn away, embarrassed and frightened by my sudden outburst of anger, and the truth I refused to accept. Images of Kafka's *Hunger Artist* flashed in my mind, and

I grew dizzy. Everything moved in slow motion, distorted somehow, like we were being pulled by some centrifugal force. It was how I'd felt as a child, on the operating table when the doctor put the anesthesia mask over my mouth and the lights grew so bright, I thought their radiance might swallow me.

Get this body out of here! my mother had yelled. Was she dreaming? Had the cancer spread to her brain? There were signs, but maybe I ignored them.

Now she was convinced she had already died, and her corpse lay before her on the bed. "You're not dead," I said again, as if trying to convince myself.

"Take my pulse then."

I took her hand in mine and pressed my finger to her wrist, where the vein bulged.

"Well?" she asked, as if she already knew the answer. When I admitted I couldn't find a pulse, she smirked. It was a look she'd given on nights in my twenties when I'd come home drunk, insisting I'd only had a beer or two. It was a look that said, "Who do you think you're talking to? I'm your mother, remember?" It was a look that said, "See, I told you so."

Cancer for Christmas Part I

Saturday, December 22, 2018

A month before my mother moved in with us, Jenny and I drove from Pittsburgh to Dunkirk to spend Christmas with her. We pulled into the parking lot of the Lincoln Arms, the complex where my mother had lived for the last five years, around 8:00 p.m. Snow covered the icy pavement. The moon was full.

The stench of cigarette smoke assaulted us as soon as the elevator doors opened onto the fourth floor. My mother's apartment was at the end of the hallway. On her door, a sticker of Pope Francis greeted us—along with one that read *Jesus Was a Refugee.*

Her one-bedroom apartment was cluttered with furniture and memorabilia—Elvis, the Kennedys, and Jesus. A black-and-white portrait of John Lennon, which I painted in high school, hung on the wall to the left. There were also several portraits my uncle Joe had painted—one of Robert Kennedy, and one of my great-grandfather, Giuseppe, sitting on a crate, smoking a corn cob pipe. The television stood on top of a bookshelf in the left corner near the sliding glass door. Next to it was a tiny Christmas tree decorated with white lights with presents underneath.

I turned on a dim lamp. All the lights in my mother's apartment burned dimly, making me feel as if I were trapped inside a Rembrandt painting.

In the tiny kitchen, the green digits of the stove's clock glowed. I checked the fridge and freezer to find a few TV dinners, popsicles, an opened package of Italian sausage, a half-eaten bowl of Bob Evans mashed potatoes, orange juice, and a quart of milk past its expiration—all the groceries I had bought on my last visit two weeks earlier.

Then I called out to my mother. When she didn't answer I called again. Walking through the living room, I nudged her bedroom door open to find a mound of sheets and blankets piled atop her bed.

Suddenly, the tangle of sheets started to move, and the outline of her face came into focus.

"Hello?" My mother's voice creaked like a rusty hinge. I moved closer, searching in the half dark.

"Everything hurts," she groaned. "My hips. My arms, my legs."

*

My mother didn't often go to the doctor. Like me, she wasn't keen on taking advice about her health or lifestyle. In November she'd fallen on a couple different occasions and bounced hard on the living room floor. *Fainting spells*, she called them.

"I was walking into my bedroom, and *Boom*!" she told me over the phone. The next thing she remembered was lying on the floor.

I admit I was worried, but didn't pressure her to call her doctor. I knew she wouldn't. She also wouldn't stand for my threats, or my nagging. She was an adult, she'd say. She was her own person.

That same month, Jenny and I visited to celebrate her 75th birthday and announce that we had decided, after living together for four years, to get married. My uncle Joe and aunt Stephanie came over with two bottles of champagne to help us celebrate.

After dinner, my mother collapsed. I held her hand as she lay on the floor, and we waited for the ambulance. Her eyes rolled back in her head, and she vomited.

By the time the EMTs arrived, she had recovered and was sitting on the couch. We told them about her other episodes. One of the EMTs took my mother's hand and said, "Fainting isn't normal, deary." There was nothing I could do or say to convince my mother to go to the ER that night, but being called *deary* only strengthened her resolve to stay home.

*

I knew my mother would want to stay home now, three nights before Christmas, as I watched her pull herself into a sitting position, but each movement caused her to cry out.

"Why didn't you say something on the phone?" I asked, though I knew the answer. We talked about the things we always talked about: the news, my job (which I hated), what was happening in Dunkirk, and how my aunt and uncle were doing. But her private medical affairs, she'd tell me, were her own business.

Jenny, who was standing behind me, suggested that having a doctor check her out might be a good idea, that going now might be better than waiting until Christmas. Maybe all she needed was something for the pain.

"I'm not going to the emergency room," she said, wincing. I could see the tightness of her jaw, the rigidness in which she held herself at the edge of the bed.

I felt the urge to scream, to order her to get dressed and get into the car so I could drive her to the hospital. But who was I to make demands? I also knew she didn't want the ambulance to come only to have the other residents—busy-bodies, she called them—gawking at her from behind their half-opened doors.

After a few moments, she caught her breath and, looking at me with a new sense of urgency, pointed a crooked finger in the direction of the living room.

"Open your presents!" she commanded. "Now! Before it's too late!"

With great effort, she managed to get out of bed and settle in her favorite chair. Jenny and I opened our presents: a gallon jug of Carlo Rossi Paisano, a bag of popcorn, and a twelve-pack of Blue Moon beer. In a white envelope I found a card with a gift certificate for two nights at a local B&B.

"It's for tonight," she said. "You have to check in by ten o'clock."

It was a nice gift, and practical. Her apartment was really too small for the three of us. But I wasn't sure it was a good idea. Jenny and I had made plans to meet up with my two oldest friends, Mike and Vin, at a local bar, but we were tired from the drive, and worried about my mother. I didn't want to leave my mother alone, especially after seeing the state she was in.

"Go," my mother said, as if reading my mind. "I'll be okay."

She lit a cigarette and turned on the television. "Hang On Sloopy" blasted from the oldies station.

"I probably just fractured my hip," she said, as if a fractured hip was nothing at all. It could wait until after the holidays, or forever as far as she was concerned.

The Likes of Me

1971

My parents had been married for two years, eight months, and twenty-eight days when I arrived at 8:49 p.m. on a Saturday in July 1971. I had blue eyes, curly red hair, and numerous, life-threatening birth defects. At full term, I weighed just three pounds, eleven ounces—about the weight of ten avocados, or your average ring-tailed lemur.

When my mother went into labor, my parents were in Jamestown, New York, a town known for furniture manufacturing and the birthplace of Lucille Ball. My father dropped her off at WCA Hospital and then went to buy lottery tickets. Maybe, as he drove, he heard Jerry Reed singing "When You're Hot, You're Hot" on the car radio. Maybe he hoped that the day his first child was born would be a lucky one. Did my mother, as she lay on a gurney, alone in the hospital, recite the Hail Mary, or pray to Saint Teresa, her favorite saint? Father Bernardo had told her that bringing a child into the world was the only reason for her and my father to marry. Whether or not this story was apocryphal, I'm certain neither my father nor mother were in any way prepared for the likes of me.

According to my mother, after delivering me, Dr. Dickson sat down and wept. A priest was summoned to perform the sacrament of last rites so that if I died, I wouldn't be cast into everlasting limbo. Then I was rushed by ambulance to Buffalo's Children's Hospital, some seventy miles away. My mother had lost a lot of blood, gone into obstetric shock and didn't even get the chance to hold me.

During my first days of life, I underwent several emergency surgeries. Like the Six Million Dollar Man, who was to become one of my childhood heroes, I had a team of doctors and nurses working to rebuild me.

Among my abnormalities was something called esophageal atresia. My upper and lower esophagus were not connected, like in Michelangelo's *The Creation of Adam,* where God's hand and Adam's reach out for one another but never touch. A section of my large intestines was also missing, I had no kidney on my left side, a double kidney on my right side, and a bladder that didn't work. Thus, I was unable to take in any nourishment or expel any waste.

To repair my esophagus, Dr. Theodore Jewett had to cut me nearly in half and stretch the two sections of my esophagus to close the gap. Though the surgery was a success, my esophagus kept constricting, and I was still unable to eat or drink. Dr. Jewett was forced to make an incision in my left side, just below my ribcage, and insert a feeding tube. He also performed a colostomy and put a stoma (an opening fashioned from my small intestines) on the left side of my stomach, which looked like a dab of Heinz ketchup.

Another surgeon, Dr. Joseph Dwoskin, a urologist, set to work on my neurogenic bladder. Due to underdevelopment and/or nerve damage, signals from my brain telling my bladder that it was full were either never sent or never reached their destination. He drilled two tiny holes into my right side and rerouted my ureters, connecting my double kidney to these two holes and bypassing my non-functioning bladder. This was called an ileostomy. He informed my mother that there was nothing else to be done, that there was not another urologist alive who could do better. It would be through those two tiny holes that I peed. Thus, I was doomed to be in diapers for the rest of my life.

If that wasn't enough, there was also my left leg, which was shorter than my right, with a knee that bent sideways like an elbow. I had no subtalar joint, which meant I could not move my ankle. From the knee down, my leg lacked any muscle and looked like the slim end of a Louisville Slugger. At the end of this, a four-toed clubfoot sprouted, like a hunk of ginger root or coral.

Most of my abnormalities could be found on the left side of my body. In addition to my deformed left leg, I had three missing ribs, and bones missing from my left hand. I'd find out at the age of eight or nine that I had a lazy left eye. It was as if construction workers assigned to building the infrastructure of my body during gestation just up and left one day, leaving me incomplete. Even my heart was on the wrong side. In fact, I'd eventually find out that it was not only on my right side, but nearly wedged into my shoulder.

Was this the happy future my parents imagined when they were pronounced husband and wife? Was this their American Dream?

If you'd have asked my mother, she'd have told you my birth defects were her fault, a guilt she carried like a millstone her entire life.

In January 1971, my mother was involved in a minor car accident and had X-rays. This, she claimed, is when she found out she was pregnant. Doctors would come to believe that the X-rays were the cause of my deformities.

My father, if you got him talking, would also blame my mother and go on to tell you about the curse he believed had been cast on him long ago. It was this curse, he reasoned, that prevented his so-called ship from coming in. It was why, no matter how hard he tried, he could never get ahead.

"In the early modern period, monstrous births were interpreted as signs, or omens from God," writes Dr. Alan W. Bates, MD, PhD, Honorary Senior Lecturer in Pathology at University College London. The mother was most often blamed for her perceived lapses in moral order.

In the Gospel of John, however, Jesus rebukes these claims, telling his disciples that children born with serious physical deformities happen *so the works of God might be displayed in them.* Despite her feelings of guilt, my mother would no doubt have agreed with Jesus.

Doctors, she'd say, informed her that the large quantity of water and amniotic fluid she retained preserved me and kept me alive inside her. Was this true, or had my mother created this story as a way to lessen her own sense of guilt? Didn't amniotic fluid protect all babies in the womb? Maybe she believed it was God's will that I survived and it was her cross to bear to protect me.

*

Before my arrival, my parents, Richard and Audrey Irwin, lived a typical small-town American life. They enjoyed long bicycle rides, antiquing, playing Canasta, and spending time with family. They watched primetime television, believed in God and the righteousness of America.

If you looked through their wedding album, you'd see a couple in love. Take, for example, the mischievous look in my mother's eyes as she shoves a slice of cake in my father's mouth, or the one of them standing outside the church, my father beaming with an awkward, almost embarrassed pride.

They met in the mid-60s, at a bowling alley in Dunkirk, the same bowling alley where, years earlier, my mother smoked her first cigarette. About their meeting, my mother wrote in her journal: *Rich wore Bermuda shorts. He was very handsome and was a good dancer.*

My father grew up on a farm in Barcelona, New York, a spit of land on the southern shore of Lake Erie, just outside of Westfield, famous for Concord grapes and Welch's grape juice. It is also the birthplace of Grace Bedell, who as a young girl wrote to Abraham Lincoln and told him he'd look much better with whiskers. There's a statue in a park where the town's movie theater once stood, commemorating their meeting in February 1861, during Lincoln's inaugural journey to Washington, D.C.

Eighteen miles west of Dunkirk, my father's family farmed the land until the state of New York seized it in 1951 through eminent domain for the construction of the I-90 Thruway. The house, one of the first Sears Modern Homes—a series of pre-fab houses—was moved a half mile up the road, to where it still stands today.

As a teenager, my father worked for Westfield Fisheries, delivering fish around the county. He also worked in construction along with his father, helping to build the Robert Moses Power Plant in Lewiston, New York, which opened in 1961. Then he was drafted into the U.S. Army and served until 1965, just missing Lyndon Baines Johnson's troop surge in Vietnam.

My mother, named after the comic strip character *Little Audrey*, grew up in a modest two-story house in Dunkirk. She was the second child of Mike and Elizabeth Rhoda, whose parents emigrated from Italy in the first decade of the 20th century.

Her older brother Joe was an artist and, like The Six Million Dollar Man, was one of my first heroes. As a teenager, my mother worked at the candy counter at The Capitol Theater. She also volunteered at Saint Joseph's Home for Exceptional Children. True to her stubbornness and extreme empathy, she quit after an argument with a nun who refused to allow her to bring one of the children home with her for Christmas dinner. No stranger to health problems, throughout her own childhood and into early adulthood she suffered from anemia and scoliosis, endured hospitalizations, and even wore a back brace and cast for long periods of time.

Three years after she graduated from high school, my mother moved to the Washington, D.C. area during the summer of 1964, after landing a job as a medical transcriptionist at Suburban Hospital in Bethesda. Later she worked as an office clerk at the U.S. Chamber of Commerce. It was no small feat for a young, single woman in those days, leaving the small-town life behind for the big city—a courageous step toward autonomy.

By the time my parents met at the bowling alley, they were both back living and working in their hometowns—my father at Reynolds, a factory that built gears for New York City subway cars, and my mother as a medical transcriptionist at Brooks Hospital. Though they were both registered Republicans, my mother worshipped the Kennedys and Martin Luther King, Jr. My father, however, blamed JFK for his being drafted and believed MLK was a communist out to destroy America. What did this mismatched couple hope their lives would be like? Did they want a big family? Did they dream of vacations in Florida or Hawaii? Regardless of what they wanted, they got me.

I've often wondered how my parents reacted the first time they laid eyes on me. Did they shudder the way the protagonist,

Henry, in David Lynch's film *Eraserhead* shuddered, as he unwrapped the bandages that hid his son like a mummy, only to reveal a creature part reptile, part alien—a head without a body, just a mass of organs and blood that spilled out like soup? Did disappointment spread across their faces like a rash? Did they hold each other? Did they cry? For me? For themselves? For a life that would never be the same.

Sometimes, I envision it like a scene from a movie. Wide shot—a windowless office. The camera pans left to right. A faint whiff of aftershave and ether permeates the stale air. Framed photos of the doctor with his wife and children hang from the wood-paneled walls, along with certificates and degrees. Photos of a fishing trip, perhaps, or the doctor and his wife posing next to the Colosseum in Rome.

Cut to a closeup of the doctor—a middle-aged white man with unkempt eyebrows and deep lines, like dried up rivulets carved into his face. He's sitting behind an imposing desk, wearing an outdated tie. My parents sit across from him in matching leather chairs. My mother, still dazed from going into shock, stares at a point behind the doctor's left ear, while my father's unblinking grey-green eyes focus on the carpet in front of him.

"We have to be realistic," the doctor might have said, his metallic, monotone voice spooling out like some foreign language. "There's a strong possibility your son will be an imbecile, that he'll need constant care for the rest of his life, that is, presuming of course, that he survives." My parents nod their heads in bewilderment.

In moments of self-loathing, I try to imagine what my parents' life would have been without me in it. Maybe if I'd died in the ambulance as I was being rushed from Jamestown to Buffalo, or during one of my emergency surgeries, my parents' lives would have been less stressful; maybe they would have been happier, remained married, and would have even gone on to have more children. Maybe my mother would have spoken my name on the anniversary of my birth, or on Christmas Eve, perhaps, when they opened their stocking gifts—turning me into an angel who was born so sick and tiny that God called him home.

Cancer for Christmas Part II

Sunday, December 23, 2018

Jenny and I had met up with my friends at Rookie's bar, and after about an hour we left. I drove Jenny to the B&B and then went back to my mother's apartment. When I returned, my mother was asleep. I undressed and lay on the couch with a blanket pulled over my head. Around 2:30 a.m., she woke me, calling from her room. The pain in her hips and legs had returned and she needed help getting to the bathroom.

"Just let me sit a minute," she said on her way back to bed, resting on a chair to catch her breath. After a few minutes she asked me to bring her cigarettes, a lighter, and an ashtray. At two-thirty she still didn't have the strength to stand. After a second cigarette, she agreed to let me call an ambulance.

In the emergency room, we waited for hours to see the sole doctor on duty. We were taken to a windowless room at the end of the hall. It was cold and dirty. Dust motes and blood-stained band-aids lay under the bed.

As it happened, the doctor was the same man who had treated my mother a few months earlier when Jenny and I brought her to the ER for foot pain. Back then, the doctor had ordered X-rays to make sure it wasn't something far worse than bunions or arthritis. My mother grew restless while waiting and insisted we leave before the doctor returned with her results.

Now, after he examined my mother, the doctor again ordered X-rays and a CT scan. Time passed, and my mother's impatience once again boiled. Every few minutes she directed me to walk down the hall to look for the doctor, who was nowhere in sight.

"I told you this place sucks," she said. "Let's get the fuck out of here."

I sat in a hard-backed chair and laughed to myself. Since her stroke, my mother had told lots of people to fuck off: the office that sent home-health aides to her apartment, pharmacists, physical therapists, and the people at the cable company. Especially the people at the cable company.

"If I was sick," I said, "You'd make me stay."

"That's different. I'm your mother."

"So?"

"Sew buttons," she spat.

*

Finally, at 7:30 in the morning, after four hours of waiting, the doctor walked into the room. He wiped his brow with the back of his hand and sat down in a chair next to my mother. He had that wild, disheveled look of an insomniac or speed freak.

"Well," he said, then paused as if the words were stuck somewhere deep in his throat and he had to draw them out slowly.

"Well, what?" my mother snapped.

"How are you feeling? How's your pain?"

"I'm cranky and I wanna go home," she said. "I want a cigarette."

The doctor reached out to touch my mother's hand, only to have her jerk it away. Conscious of this failed moment of tenderness, the doctor rested his hands on his knees and took a deep breath.

"You have cancer," he proclaimed, as if he were telling my mother that she had a pimple, or a rash. "You have cancer," he said again and looked at me. That's when the ground gave way like a trapdoor in a cartoon, and all three of us—me, my mother, and the doctor—plummeted to our separate and communal doom. At the same time I felt my throat begin to close and my legs and arms stiffen. I watched my mother's brow tighten, then jump in surprise. For the briefest moment, our eyes locked. Then, as she looked away, she began to shrink. It was as if she were sinking into the sheets, withdrawing into herself. It was like I was looking at her through the wrong end of a telescope.

"It's not a fractured hip?" my mother asked, after a moment.

"No," the doctor replied. "You have tumors on your pelvis and lower spine."

How could he speak so calmly? Had he forgotten it was the day before Christmas Eve? Didn't he realize we had to get home to have coffee and listen to Christmas songs? To cook those frozen hors d'oeuvres my mother loved—little quiches and hot dogs wrapped in pastry dough? Didn't he know my aunt Stephanie was cooking dinner?

"You have cancer," the doctor said. And I was a child again, thinking about all those Christmases past, how excited my mother used to be, even more excited than I was. I thought about how she'd hang an Advent calendar in the dining room, and inside each little door, place a gift for me to open on the corresponding day. I thought of how she used to paint the four windows in the dining room: a snowman, a Christmas tree, Santa Claus, the Virgin Mary holding the baby Jesus. I thought of the times we drove around town, looking at all the lights and decorations people hung around their houses, houses on Taft Place, Jerboa Street, and Shore Acres, and the mansion where the owner of Dunkirk Ice Cream lived, with its ice-cream-cone-shaped wrought iron gates strung with white lights and giant candy canes.

Every year after we finished decorating our Christmas tree, my mother would turn off all the lights in the house and sit staring at it for hours. When I was a senior in high school, working my first job as a cashier at Tops grocery store, I saved up $100 and bought my mother a new artificial tree. We placed it near the front door, so no matter what room you entered from, it was the first thing you saw. It was magnificent.

My mother cut construction paper to look like the bricks, logs, and flames of a fireplace, and taped them onto the island in the center of our kitchen. Above this she hung our stockings. She always made sure I had gifts to open. Even if she didn't have money to pay the gas or electric bill, she always found money for Christmas. "We can open one stocking gift," she'd say, but after she opened her gift, she'd want to open them all, the ones in the stocking and the ones under the tree!

When the emergency room doctor pushed back his chair, I was jolted from my memories. He stood for a moment in silence, then told my mother and me how sorry he was. He recommended that she make an appointment with her primary care physician as soon as possible, as well as with an oncologist at Roswell—the cancer hospital in Buffalo where, as it happened, both my mother's parents had been patients when I was in high school. My grandfather survived breast cancer surgery, but my nana succumbed to a tumor in her kidney that metastasized to her lungs and brain.

Part of me always knew this moment would arrive. Yet I imagined that day was far off in the distant future. To my shock, it appeared like a storm cloud sweeping in off the horizon, catching us unawares.

My Mother's Little Red Book

1971-1975

Because of all my health problems I needed around-the-clock care. This forced my mother to quit her job as a medical transcriptionist. While my father at least had the escape that his work provided, as well as the solitary eighteen miles he drove back and forth each day, my mother was stuck with me 24/7. She took me to all my doctor's appointments, and whenever I was admitted to the hospital she stayed in my room, sleeping on two hard-back chairs pushed together, or a fold-out cot the nurses provided.

She chronicled it all in the pages of a little red book—all my surgeries and hospitalizations, my immunizations, my growth, as well as all my little milestones, which seemed even more exceptional, considering the grim prognoses my doctors spouted like doomsday fortune tellers. Thankfully, my father had top-notch health insurance. According to my mother, it covered everything, and they never received a bill. These were the days before high deductibles and copayments, before HMOs required referrals and restricted patients to in-network doctors and hospitals.

I arrived home from the hospital for the first time on September 17, 1971, two months to the day after I was born, with a cast over my left leg, and a gastric feeding tube sticking out of the left side of my gut. The tube forced me to sleep sitting up. Three days later it popped out and my parents had to drive me back to Children's Hospital in Buffalo, so doctors could reinsert it into the gaping hole just below my left nipple. This scene would repeat itself over and over during the next year: my parents driving frantically while I screamed and cried. It could happen at 1:00 p.m. in the middle of *All My Children*, or just as my mother had served dinner to my father, who hadn't even had a chance to take off his work clothes. Finally, on June 19, 1972, after almost a year, the tube was removed for the last time.

Between the pages of the red book, on a folded sheet of lined paper torn from a tablet, my mother listed my 26 abnormalities. Highlights from this list included esophageal atresia and urinary tract abnormalities, as well as deformity of the left chest, agenesis of the lower half of the sacral spine and multiple abnormalities of vertebrae D-8 and D-9.

Defying my orthopedic doctor's expectations, who told my mother there was a good chance I'd never walk, I took my first steps a week before my second birthday. After that, I was sent to Alex Campanella, who fit me with a brace. His clinic was located in the dingy basement of Children's Hospital. The brace was constructed of two metal rods that splinted my left leg up to my groin with two leather harnesses—one at my thigh and one at my knee. My parents had to buy special orthopedic shoes at a store in Buffalo, one size for my right foot and a smaller size for my club foot. Attached to the bottom of the smaller shoe was a six-inch cork lift.

I hated those shit-brown shoes. They reminded me of shoes my grandfather wore, though today they'd be fashionable. All my left-pant legs had to be shortened, and a zipper sewn in because they wouldn't fit over my lift otherwise. My grandmother Irwin, an expert sewer, was commissioned for this task. In addition to altering my pants, she created beautiful afghans and quilts, and one year for Halloween made me a King Kong costume.

*

My grandmother Irwin also gave my parents money for a down payment on a three-bedroom house. On Saint Patrick's Day, 1972, during a blizzard, the three of us and our dog Moses moved into 620 Main Street in Dunkirk. Our house, built in 1910, was army green with a large front porch, drop ceilings, and no insulation. Faux wood paneling covered the dining room walls, and the kitchen had bright yellow linoleum floors and flowery wallpaper. There was a one-car driveway and backyard with a maple tree and room enough for a swing set, a vegetable garden, and a clubhouse, which my father would build out of two-by-fours and plywood.

From the outside looking in, life was good, or nearly so. The average annual income was $11,800. Gas cost 55 cents a gallon. The Watergate hearings aired on TV, prisoners rioted at Attica, the Lakota occupied Wounded Knee, and the OPEC oil crisis was waiting in the wings, but these events had little if any effect on our lives. We were just another cookie-cutter family, on a street full of cookie-cutter families—a taciturn man, his effervescent, opinionated wife, a neurotic dog who refused to be housebroken, and their curly-haired firstborn child who had Frankensteinian scars crisscrossing his deformed body.

If photographs from that time reflect an honest portrait of my life, they showed that despite my birth defects, I was a happy baby. Take for example the photo of my mother and me on the day of my baptism: I'm dressed all in white, staring bug-eyed at the camera. My mother is wearing a blue-patterned mini-dress, her black hair in a shag. There's a photo from my first birthday, where my father holds my tiny body cautiously, as if he's afraid I'll break. In another, I pose with my right arm raised, my index finger pointing to the sky like an exclamation mark, as if that was what I was supposed to do anytime someone took my picture. “Here I am,” it said, “Look at me!” Yet, like all babies and toddlers, I was greedy and inconsiderate, ignorant of the stress my very presence caused my parents and the strain it put on their lives, and their marriage.

In those years, my mother and I spent countless hours at doctor’s offices and in hospitals, where I underwent a barrage of tests. There were blood tests and IVs. Always needles—terrible, frightening needles. In some tests I was made to lie perfectly still on a cold metal table as a giant machine hovered above me like a spaceship, taking snapshots of my esophagus, kidney, bladder, and leg. Another test involved drinking a chalky milkshake spiked with radioactive dye. On a grainy black-and-white screen, I watched it travel down the narrow road of my esophagus.

My nana, my maternal grandmother, always accompanied us on these day-long outings. She doted on me, smothered me in her perfumed kisses and talked to me in her garbled baby talk. With my father at work, my mother needed someone at her side, a companion she could unload her frustrations on, someone sympathetic, someone willing to pay for lunch or gas for the car. My nana was that person.

Amid all this, my parents sued Brooks Hospital, believing what my doctors at Children’s Hospital believed: that my deformities were caused by radiation from X-rays my mother received after a fender bender in January 1971. My mother claimed she didn’t know she was pregnant. “Back then they weren’t required to put a lead shield over you,” she told me. “It wasn’t until our case that New York State made it a law.”

I’ve searched the internet but could find nothing that mentioned me or my mother, or any law that required hospitals to cover pregnant women, or women who thought they might be pregnant, with lead aprons. One article, however, said that lead aprons had been recommended since the 1950s.

Complicating matters, there were times my mother told me that she realized she was pregnant as far back as November 1970, when she became ill at the baptism of a friend's daughter and threw up in the baptismal font.

Regardless, we were awarded $50,000—to be put in trust until I turned twenty-one. The money would be used to pay for any future medical expenses. Since my father was a man, as well as the chief breadwinner, not to mention his belief that he was an expert on investing and the stock market (though there was no evidence to support these claims), he was charged with overseeing the trust. Decades into the future this would cause a rift in our lives that would never be fully repaired.

Once, I asked my mother how she and my father managed—all my hospitalizations and surgeries, the driving back and forth to Buffalo, the sleepless nights. "It was just something we did," she said.

People who knew the intimate details of my deformities (my doctors, my mother, a few nurses) or those who had a somewhat lesser and oftentimes misguided knowledge (my father, my aunt and uncle, my grandparents) might say it was nothing short of a miracle that I survived, that surely God had been watching over me. Maybe, but I have no desire to be a poster child or anyone's inspiration. Had you asked me when I was ten or eleven, I might've told you I was destined for greatness. Why else had I survived? At sixteen or seventeen, I might have said that I was doomed, that God, if he existed, was trying to kill me. I realize now that there was nothing miraculous except that I felt for the most part like a normal child. Besides, what other life did I have to compare with?

Dr. Akkinepally

Thursday, December 27, 2018

Two days after Christmas, Jenny and I took my mother to see her primary care physician, Dr. Sita Lakshmi Akkinepally. I pushed my mother into the doctor's office with the wheelchair a friend had lent her. She'd had the chair for a few years, but pride had prevented her from allowing anyone, especially the other residents at the Lincoln Arms, to see her being pushed around like an old lady or an invalid. The fact that she agreed to use the chair now only proved the severity of her pain.

The waiting room was full of mostly elderly patients, hunched over, dressed in heavy winter coats and scarves. My eyes were drawn to the television where a mindless, late-morning talk show was playing. Thankfully, the sound was turned off. Sitting there, I found myself whispering the Lord's Prayer, even though I'd lost faith at sixteen.

Ten minutes passed before a nurse called my mother's name and ushered the three of us into a small exam room. Before long Dr. Akkinepally arrived. She was dressed in a yellow sweater and knee-high boots. I remembered meeting her a year earlier when I brought my mother to an appointment. She was in her thirties, intelligent and caring, and spoke to the point. My mother had her share of doctors who didn't return phone calls, doctors who were either clueless, or just didn't give a damn. Dr. Akkinepally was not one of them.

After going over my mother's long list of health problems (hypothyroidism, high blood pressure, anemia, arthritis, insomnia, scoliosis, and recurring bronchitis, as well as the lingering effects of her stroke), the doctor reminded my mother of the many times she'd refused to submit to tests (mammograms, colonoscopies, CT scans). I wondered if this was said more for my benefit than hers.

A year earlier, my mother had agreed to schedule a CT scan. I told her I'd get off work and take her, but she said not to worry and that her friend Jackie would do it.

"It'll give us an excuse to hang out," she said. "We'll go to lunch afterwards, make a day of it."

When I called the day of the appointment, she told me it had been canceled. She never rescheduled. Since her stroke, it had become a battle to convince my mother to keep her doctor's appointments, but I tried not to push. "I'm not a child," she'd say, in that low biting tone she employed whenever she felt her sovereignty threatened.

In the end, I let it go. It was easier than arguing, easier than taking off work and driving three hours each way. It was easier for both of us to pretend to forget about it: *it* being the possibility that something major was wrong, something we were both too afraid to confront.

Now, after examining my mother, who remained sitting in the wheelchair, Dr. Akkinepally repeated what the emergency room doctor had said: "You have cancer."

"It's in your bones," she said. "But more than likely it originated somewhere else."

This "somewhere else," she guessed was in the blood, or the lungs, since my mother had been a heavy smoker since she was eighteen. Yet there was no way to be certain without a biopsy.

My mother didn't want a biopsy. She didn't need to know where the cancer originated. "Is it going to make a difference?" she hissed. "I don't think so." Fortunately Dr. Akkinepally understood my mother's proclivities, how stubborn she was, how determined she was to hang on to her independence, as well as her cigarettes.

I don't remember Dr. Akkinepally telling my mother she didn't have to have the MRI that the emergency room doctor ordered. I don't remember her talking about alternative options—hospice or palliative care. I don't remember her asking my mother if she wanted the head oncologist in the area to review the ER report and CT scan results. All this, Jenny would tell me later.

Just like in the ER, a few nights earlier, I felt a wave of nausea overtake me and I began to sweat. The fluorescent lights swirled and dimmed. The room grew foggy, and I felt as if I were falling. The doctor's words sounded like a weather forecast: *A cold front is moving in. Your mother has cancer. The next ten days will be cloudy. She will die soon.*

My mother did not respond or even look at the doctor. Why didn't I say something? Or my mother? Did she just plan to sit around and wait to die? I sat like a zombie, picking my fingernails until the flesh around them bled—a habit from childhood that resurfaced whenever I was stressed or anxious.

"You shouldn't live alone anymore," I heard Dr. Akkinepally say as the fog around me lifted.

"We want Audrey to move in with us," Jenny announced.

"Do I have to decide now?" my mother asked. The exasperation in her voice was clear, as was the fear.

*

In the parking lot, as I helped my mother into the car, I wondered what would have happened if Jenny and I had gone to Jenny's parents for Christmas. Would my mother have told anyone she wasn't able to get out of bed? Or would she have kept it a secret, lying there, waiting to die? Hoping to die?

What would it be like living with her again? I'd asked her to move to Pittsburgh many times, assuring her she wouldn't be a burden. But did I really mean it? Hadn't I always felt a sense of relief each time she refused? Jenny and I were trying to make a life together, trying to be writers while holding down day jobs. We had our routines, our favorite restaurants and bars and record stores. Did I value record stores more than my mother?

I also thought of my nana, who died of cancer when I was a senior in high school. The rounds of chemo and radiation she suffered through did not stop the cancer, and she spent the last weeks of her life in a coma. I knew my mother did not want that to happen to her, and neither did I.

What Can You Do?

Thursday, December 27, 2018

After we returned to her apartment, my mother settled into her favorite spot on the couch. I walked to the pharmacy across the street and picked up the hydrocodone Dr. Akkinepally had prescribed. Afterward, I stood on the balcony, gazing out over Main Street. On the corner there was a Rent-A-Center where the convenience store I had once worked at used to be. One Christmas Eve, a house caught fire a half block from the store and a little boy died. They said it was a faulty heater. I could smell the smoke every time the door opened.

This was once my world, I thought, looking across a derelict expanse. These streets, this town, named for another in France, built and abandoned by the railroad and steel industry and the false promises of Urban Renewal—this was once my life, the one I fled seventeen years earlier when I went off to graduate school. Now I'd become a stranger here, just someone vaguely familiar, passing through.

I turned and watched Jenny and my mother through the sliding glass door. I couldn't hear what they were saying, but I could see their facial expressions: pantomimes of worry and disbelief.

A few days after my mother's stroke, while she was still in the hospital in Erie, I was alone in her apartment and found the obituary she'd written for herself on the kitchen table. I wondered if she'd written it while waiting for the ambulance.

Audrey Rhoda Irwin, it read, *was called home today by Jesus Christ*. Her instructions were clear. She didn't want a wake or funeral. Instead, she asked that people do an act of kindness in her name. She also decided to donate her body to science; there was a brochure from the University of Buffalo's Anatomical Society. I knew her decision was partly about money. Jenny and I weren't destitute—we earned enough for rent, our car payment, pizza on the weekends—but I bought our wedding bands at a pawn shop. By donating her body, my mother was trying to spare us an expense she knew we couldn't afford.

*

Inside the apartment, I poured a cup of coffee and sat across from my mother and Jenny. What would the next few weeks have in store for us, I wondered. Would Jenny and I have to postpone our wedding? Would we be able to convince my mother to move to Pittsburgh? My medical problems had always taken precedence, determining the trajectory of our days and nights. Now, my mother's took center stage.

"I really thought Dr. Akkinepally was gonna tell me it was all a mistake," my mother said. "I thought she'd say I didn't really have cancer."

I knew she was afraid. *I* was afraid. But as was her way, she put up a good front, smiling in the face of her own demise.

"Well," she announced, after a long silence, "I guess I better call your uncle and tell him the news."

On the phone she spoke matter-of-factly, as if she were addressing a child. "What can you do, Joey?" she said. "That's life. We can't change it."

Among the Dead

My mother lived among the dead her entire life. She saw ghosts from a young age. "They're not something to be feared," she once told me. The dead were watching out for us. Sometimes they just wanted to make sure we didn't forget them.

As a child, my mother often saw an old woman pass by the living room window outside my grandparents' house. The woman was tall and stout, and wore her white hair tied in a bun. Each time she passed—walking with a slow determination down the narrow path that ran from the front porch to the backyard—my mother would clop through the house, her heart pounding with anticipation. But by the time she made her way through the kitchen door and out onto the porch, the woman had vanished. No one else ever saw her, and my mother kept this apparition to herself. She was convinced, however, that this strange woman appeared to her for a reason, like she had some message or truth she wanted to share.

Long after the mysterious old woman stopped appearing to my mother, my grandparents hung a portrait of a woman above their television. It was then, and only then, according to my mother, that she found out that the woman she'd seen passing outside the window was her grandmother, Almarinda Bartolomeo. Mary, as she was known, died in 1938, six years before my mother was born. Had she glimpsed this photo once before and forgotten it? Did her grandmother's ghost really appear, and if so, for what purpose?

Growing up Catholic and working-class in the 40s and 50s,

my mother and her older brother Joe lived a life that revolved around family and the church. They were taught to honor their parents, to say their prayers, and to always be in fear for the fate of their mortal souls. The parish priest, Father Bernardo, used to point his finger at the children, warning them that he had the power to send their souls to hell.

Faith in God and Jesus, and the promise of heaven, would remain a central part of my mother's life. Yet, guilt and superstition would also play prominent roles.

My great-aunt Rose, my nana's older sister, took care of my mother in her infancy, when her colicky crying became too much for my nana. Rose was famous among Dunkirk's close-knit Italian-American community for her ability to banish the evil eye, or *malocchio*. This old-world alchemy was achieved in various ways, including saying prayers and rubbing olive oil on the afflicted person's head and chest. Years after Rose died, my mother claimed she appeared to her in a dream and cured her of the migraines that sometimes plagued her. The dead, it seemed, were never far away.

Once, walking into work at Saint Vincent's Assisted Living Center, my mother noticed one of her favorite residents, Gerti, standing in the window of her room, waving. It wasn't anything unusual. Gerti often waited for my mother's midnight arrival before she went to bed. Sometimes she even woke at three or four in the morning and sat talking with her in the office.

That night, Jeanette, one of my mother's coworkers, was waiting for her in the vestibule.

"I see Gerti's up late tonight," my mother said.

"What do you mean?" Jeanette asked.

"I just saw her waving from her window."

"But Gerti died this afternoon!" Jeanette said. "I've been a nervous wreck waiting to tell you."

Who were these ghosts—my great-grandmother Mary, Rose, Gerti, and countless others? Were they just figments of my mother's imagination, talismans that helped her survive the unpredictability of her Cold War childhood, her marriage, and the stress of having a deformed child? Or could they be real? For most of my life, I felt beguiled by these stories. Like family lore, they added a sense of wonder and mystery.

Despite these ghosts, or maybe because of them, she possessed an unwavering faith in God, the power of prayer, and the promise of the soul's redemption in the afterlife. No wonder she spent her final days murmuring her rosary, begging Jesus to free her from this life.

"Suffering," she used to tell me, "brings you closer to God."

Coffee, Cigarettes & Grocery Lists

March 2018

One weekend in March 2018, ten months after my mother's stroke, I drove to Dunkirk to take her to the hospital for a blood test. Doctors had been trying for years to find the correct dosage of medication for her hypothyroidism. After her stroke, we learned that my mother had a "very tiny" brain aneurysm. Although "tiny" and not directly related to her hypothyroidism, this aneurysm made it even more vital that she keep all her follow-up appointments.

Since her stroke, she'd been living, as she never tired of reminding me, like a prisoner in her own apartment. Her car had died years before, and she had to rely on others for transportation and errands. The hospital had a service where a phlebotomist would go to the elderly and shut-ins' homes, but that service ended months earlier for lack of funding. So, I told my mother I'd drive up Friday after work and take her on Saturday.

That Saturday, as I stood in front of my mother, holding my car keys, she lounged on her settee, still in her pajamas, a cigarette in one hand, a cup of coffee in the other.

"Aren't you supposed to be fasting?" I asked.

"Relax," she said, half in amusement, half in exasperation. "Have some coffee."

She said she was tired, that she didn't sleep well and wasn't in the mood to get her blood taken. Besides, it was cold outside.

What frustrated me most was her reluctance to let me help her, her refusal to help herself. When I first asked if she wanted me to take her for her blood test, she told me no. She said it was a long drive, and understood if I was too busy. But of course, she didn't understand, and it wasn't okay. My mother not only wanted me to come, she expected me to.

Regardless, the blood test was out. I poured myself a cup of coffee and then, a second cup. Later that morning, my mother dictated a list of the things she wanted at the store, and I wrote them down on a sheet of paper: Haribo gummy bears (her favorite), coffee, Fritos, TV dinners, pepperoni and cheese, ramen noodles, Jell-O, all the usual suspects. Then she handed over her EBT card and a wad of twenties, which she kept stuffed in an envelope inside the cushion of her settee.

"This is for paper towels, Kleenex, and toothpaste," she said. "Oh, and an eight-piece meal with mashed potatoes and extra gravy from KFC."

For a long time, my mother received $20 per month in food stamps, and then, one month, without explanation, it went up to $194. No matter, she never came close to spending it all. So, I bought extra foods I knew she'd never buy for herself, foods she felt she didn't deserve: T-bone steaks, fresh vegetables, as well as some "healthier" TV dinners. I know that many people believe that those on welfare should not buy gummy bears, Jell-O, and T-bone steaks, but I thought my mother deserved it. She'd worked hard all her life—starting at sixteen when she was employed at the candy counter at the Capitol Theater, a job she said gave her money to buy her own clothes instead of wearing her cousin Geraldine's hand-me-downs.

If she needed something between my visits, my mother could ask her friend Jackie, or my aunt Stephanie, or use the delivery service that P&G Grocery provided. Usually, she chose to wait for me.

After I returned from the store, we sat in the living room

drinking more coffee as The Everly Brothers, Van Morrison, and Elvis played on the oldies station. I wrote out checks for bills that had accumulated since my last visit. My mother had two piles: one for bills that needed to be paid at once, like cable and internet, and one for those that could either wait or be thrown away, like her many doctor and hospital bills.

As I wrote out the checks, my mother complained about her home health aides. "They can't even scramble an egg," she said in disgust. "They don't know how to shop or clean." Some of the aides just sat on the couch and told my mother about their own problems. Some even fell asleep or bummed cigarettes off her. One asked my mother to sign her timecard, even though she wasn't staying for her shift. These aides were provided by my mother's Medicaid spend-down program. Since my mother earned too much money to qualify for regular Medicaid—$11 over the limit—she had to "buy in" to the spend-down program, paying $300 per month before her benefits kicked in. The spend-down program was designed to help people in a liminal phase—that area between complete disability and self-sufficiency—but my mother would remain in this phase, unmoored in a sea that would grow more and more turbulent with each passing year.

After all the checks were written, with the envelopes addressed and stamped, we'd go out for dinner if my mother felt up for it. On this particular visit, she did not, and even though we had a bucket of KFC, we ordered take-out: two personal pan pizzas with extra pepperoni from Pizza Hut. I offered to pay, but as usual, my mother wouldn't allow me to. "I won't eat!" she exclaimed and gave me that look that said she was serious, that look that told me not to even bother. It was her checkmate.

This scene played out between us over and over, the way I

remember it playing out between my mother and nana when I was a child. We had this game where we'd give each other money secretly. She'd hide money in my duffel bag, pants pocket, or in the pages of whatever book I happened to be reading—a few twenties, a fifty. In turn, I'd put money in the freezer, in the basket that sat on the toilet where my mother kept Kleenex and Q-tips, or in the spice rack, which she rarely if ever used (there were spices like oregano and paprika that had been there since I was a teenager). Once I was in my car, on my way back to Pittsburgh, I'd call her.

"Check in the freezer," I'd say. Sometimes, it was she who would call, telling me to check the back pocket of my jeans. It was a vicious cycle, but we enjoyed it.

*

After we finished our pizza, we settled on opposite couches while *Jeopardy!* played on the television. I read a chapter or two from the book I'd brought with me while my mother scrolled through Facebook. I wondered if she'd forgotten about having the blood test—the reason I'd driven up on a Friday night. Despite her stroke and aneurysm, my mother chain-smoked with a vengeance, maybe even more than she had before. While one cigarette smoldered in her ashtray, she fished a new one out of her case, as if she couldn't bear to be without one for even a second.

Looking back, I picture my mother alone in her apartment, waiting for my next visit. I imagine she assuaged herself with coffee and cigarettes and music. I see her sitting there gazing at her own reflection in the sliding glass door, worrying—about me, my uncle, my cousin Aiesha and her kids, about the government, about not having enough money, about dying, and the hacker—someone from California she was certain had taken over her laptop. She bided her time, for someone to call or visit, for night to fall, for a favorite TV show; she waited for something to happen, something that would either save her or send her to her grave. Sometimes it felt like she deliberately chose the latter.

Dr. Engel

1974

Dr. Dwoskin had told my mother there was nothing to be done to get me out of diapers. He said there was no doctor or surgery anywhere that would allow me to pee through my penis. Fortunately, my parents found Dr. Rainer Engel, a urologist at Johns Hopkins Hospital in Baltimore.

Born in Cologne, Germany, and named after the poet Rainer Maria Rilke, who was a friend of his father's, Dr. Engel was tall and soft-spoken. He had a broad forehead and high cheekbones and always wore a bow tie. My parents liked him at once.

In early 1974, an appointment was made, and the three of us drove to Baltimore, hoping Dr. Engel could fix my neurogenic bladder. The trip also gave us an excuse to visit our extended family—Gerald and his sister Geraldine (children of my nana's sister Rose) and their families, who lived in Bowie, Maryland. While technically my first cousins once removed, I simply called them my cousins. In years to come, in my early twenties, I'd spend a lot of time at Geraldine's house after she and her family moved to Sussex, New Jersey, trying to figure out what I wanted to do with my life. She and her husband Phil became like my second parents. Gerald would end up helping my mother out financially. With a generous spirit, he enjoyed helping many family members and friends in any way he could.

Dr. Engel discussed various options with my parents and suggested I return for a series of tests. On March 2, my mother wrote in her little red book, "Dr. Engel performed a right and left orchiopexy, moving Jason's undescended testicles into his scrotum."

In 1976, I stayed at Johns Hopkins for over a month and underwent tests to determine if my bladder could ever be functional. My mother slept, as she always did, in my hospital room on a fold-out cot. My father had to return to his job in New York, but he'd come down for long weekends. On one of those weekends, he, Phil, and Gerald went to the horse races to see Elocutionist win the Preakness Stakes. There are also photos of my mother, me, and my cousins at The Enchanted Forest amusement park, with all of us laughing.

Despite evidence of these happy moments, my only memory from those times was one of horror, and comes to me in flashes like some long-ago dream: it is one of me lying on a table, screaming and thrashing as my parents and two nurses hold me down and a doctor sticks me with a needle. Whether it was Dr. Engel or someone else, I can't be certain.

In the end, Dr. Engel could not make any headway in fixing my bladder, and suggested I return at some, yet-to-be-determined date, when it was convenient. Thus, that September, still in diapers, I started kindergarten.

School Days

1976

Dressed in a navy polyester suit and wide red tie, I burst through the double doors of Saint Elizabeth Ann Seton Elementary School, lopsided and lunging down the hallway, just out of reach of my nana's nervous grasp.

"You were so excited," my mother told me later. "You fell down three times. Nana and I had to pick you up and dust you off."

When I crossed the threshold of the kindergarten classroom, stepping on the red, white, and blue checkered floor that September morning, I was greeted by my teacher, Mrs. Helen Szczerbacki, who wore Catwoman glasses and had her long, mop-gray hair piled atop her head in an unkempt beehive.

Saint Elizabeth's was formed when Saint Mary's, a mostly Irish congregation, merged with Sacred Heart, a mostly German one, after the Diocese in its infinite wisdom shut down Sacred Heart and demolished the building. The school, an imposing three-story brick building, stood on the corner of Washington Avenue and Fourth Street, half a block from the church. It had two courtyards and a basement full of tunnels and secret passageways, where, one Halloween, my classmates and I were led into a dark, cobwebbed room by our teacher to see a mummy that, we were told, came all the way from "Ancient Egypt." In these depths, it was also rumored the priests and nuns met for illicit purposes.

Mornings in Mrs. Szczerbacki's class, away from my mother, didn't cause me the least bit of stress. This, I am certain, was due to the joint efforts of the teachers and staff, the priests, the ladies who worked in the cafeteria, and the new principal, Ms. Wagner, who looked like a movie star. They all went out of their way to make me feel like I belonged. They made me feel safe and loved. I imagine these mornings also gave my mother some much-needed alone time.

Kindergarten was also where I first met Mike Pakulski, who would remain a lifelong friend. On Halloween that year, we both showed up dressed as Batman. Yet Mike insisted, since he was taller, that he was the real Batman, and I, Batboy. I was about to give him a good kick to the shin with the lift of my shit-colored brace, which I would employ as a trusted weapon time and again on friend and foe alike, but Mrs. Szczerbacki intervened, and no blood was spilled. I also met Janice and Barbie, who were my first girlfriends. I'd invite them to my house for dinner on different nights, or after school to play, wooing them with my drawing skills and my Six Million Dollar Man action figure.

During recess, while the teacher's aide took my classmates to the bathroom and the water fountain, Mrs. Szczerbacki changed my diapers. In the years to follow, my mother would come to school to change them, setting me on a table in one of the girls' restrooms, while students came in and out, as if it was the most normal thing in the world.

Before all of this could happen, however, before I could be registered for classes, my mother had to go up against the totalitarian overlords of the Catholic education system. In particular, the outgoing principal, Sister Maurine—a squat, fire-breathing monster—suggested that because of my disabilities, I should be institutionalized.

As my mother and Sister Maurine screamed at one another over a desk strewn with papers, I sat in a wooden chair, my legs dangling six inches above the floor, transfixed by the crucifix that hung on the wall above Sister Maurine's head. There were framed photos of Sister Maurine with various priests and nuns, as well as with the bishop. There was even a portrait of John F. Kennedy—the same one that sat on a shelf next to my mother's paperbacks at our house.

"Don't you think the child would be better off in an institution that is more equipped to handle his needs?" Sister Maurine asked, her voice rising in pitch on the word *equipped.*

"An institution?" my mother cried. "What do you mean exactly?"

Out of the corner of my eye I saw the sister's reptilian claws clench into tiny hammers.

"His special needs," she confirmed. "I think a place with people better able to handle his..."

"He's not an animal," my mother screamed. "He doesn't need a handler."

After that, everything was a blur. All I know is that I was registered and would start kindergarten in two weeks, and Sister Maurine would retire to live out her days in the nuns' home (a former orphanage) across the street.

I often wonder what would have become of me if Sister Maurine had won the day and my mother had agreed to ship me off to some institution where people could "better handle my needs." What would have become of me if my mother hadn't given up her career as a medical transcriptionist and stayed home to care for me? What tragedies would have befallen me if my nana wasn't forever worrying over me, chasing after me as I hobbled through her kitchen, or if my grandmother Irwin didn't read me stories, or sew zippers in my pant legs? What would have happened without my grandfather's tenderness, his glowing smile. Or if my father didn't spend his days making sure the machines that built the gears for New York City subway cars worked and I could have health insurance? Wasn't I the luckiest kid in the world? (Some would say spoiled.) Wasn't I a child of God, just as my mother never tired of reminding me? Wasn't I one of his *favored?*

If you could have seen me then—arms flailing, my hair a bramble of dark curls, my amphibian eyes, one looking straight ahead, the other floating aimlessly—as I moved from point A to B with a careless disregard for the world around me, too impatient for what was next, you might have agreed with my grandmother Irwin, who referred to me as a little devil who was getting too big for his britches.

It was during those years—between the ages of five and eight—that I lived with such fearlessness, ignorant of my own fragility, that you'd think I hadn't a problem in the world. It didn't matter that I was often home sick from school, or in the hospital, or that I had to go to a speech therapist because I couldn't pronounce words with "TH" in them and called my mother "Mudder." I couldn't even pronounce my own name and called myself Josh. I doubt my parents could ever have imagined that the deformed child they brought home from the hospital, the child they had to bring back over and over again like a defective toy, would one day not only be able to live on his own, but would choose to leave them and move to some far-off city. I doubt they could have even foreseen the changes that lurked in the coming years.

My Father Moves Out

1979

"Your mother and I are going to get a separation," my father announced. It was the summer of 1979. I was eight years old. He said he and my mother needed time to figure things out, but that everything would be okay. I burst into tears even though I had no idea what getting a separation meant. Then, my father began to sing, "It's crying time again…" which only made me cry more.

What was it they needed to figure out? Was it my fault? Was it because of my esophagus? Because I was still in diapers? Was he still angry about the time I tried to flush a can of his shaving cream down the toilet?

I don't ever remember seeing my parents fight or argue. For that matter, I don't remember them showing affection toward one another either. When I think back on those years, it's like watching the trailer to a movie about someone else's life: brief flashes, fragments. My father left for work most mornings before I woke, and in the evenings, when he returned, he'd eat his dinner, which my mother prepared, and then retire to his "office" to study his stock charts and pray to the televangelist Oral Roberts for riches, as well as my healing. I didn't understand what he was doing, but at that time he was my hero, the person I thought I'd grow up to be—someone strong, someone who wore flannel shirts and a Magnum P.I. mustache, someone who walked with confidence and determination, and talked with his mouth full of potato chips.

The day he moved out—making trip after trip, carrying

boxes and piles of clothes out the kitchen door and stuffing them all inside his rusted Chevy Nova—I sat on the linoleum floor silently watching. On his last trip, he picked up our dog Moses and held him under his left arm like a football as he walked out, letting the metal screen door slam behind him.

Though I keenly felt the sudden fracture of our lives, it didn't take long for the shock and dismay of my father's departure to wear off. It wasn't that I didn't miss him, I just adapted to his not being there. Within weeks, I revised the story I only vaguely understood and turned my father into a mythic figure, a superhero, a spy. Sometimes he was off fighting some war in a country whose name I couldn't pronounce. Sometimes he was an astronaut, speeding through the galaxy. In reality, he'd moved back in with my grandmother, in the farmhouse where he grew up.

It wasn't until I was in high school that my mother said anything negative about my father. "We were always in need of money," she told me. "There were always expenses, always things we couldn't afford." She claimed my father's gambling almost lost our house.

"As soon as he got paid, he'd spend half his check on lottery tickets or some horse race down at Off Track Betting."

It was my grandmother Irwin, she said, who made the mortgage payments that he neglected.

"We wouldn't have had food," my mother claimed, "if not for Uncle Neff and Aunt Rose, who brought us groceries every week from their store." She also mentioned that my father was seeing a woman, someone who worked at a local print shop. "They used to go out drinking together," she said.

My father, in turn, would blame my mother for their divorce. If I'd asked him, he'd say he'd spent his whole life trying to get ahead, to make ends meet. If it wasn't for having to pay my medical bills, he once lamented, he'd have moved to Florida long ago.

"You know your mother used to hang around with that priest?" he said when I was a teenager, but he'd grow defensive when I questioned him. I knew he was talking about Father Doyle, who came to Saint Elizabeth's around the time my parents separated.

Father Doyle had long hair and wore round glasses. I remembered hearing rumors at school, hushed conversations. I heard enough to know that whatever was between Father Doyle and my mother at times caused her to blush with embarrassment, and other times to cry and spend long periods alone in her bedroom with the door closed. At my mother's request, Father Doyle took me out for ice cream and to play miniature golf. I went because she wanted me to go, because I'd get ice cream, but it wasn't something I'd choose to do otherwise. It wasn't that I didn't like Father Doyle, I just felt awkward and shy in his presence.

One night, walking through a stand of pine trees between the school and church, carrying a coffee can full of money from bingo, Father Doyle was robbed. The assailant, who was never identified, threw gasoline in his face. Then, a few years later, Father Doyle left the parish abruptly. Rumors again swirled, but it wasn't until I was an adult that I learned he'd been accused of molesting a boy (one of my classmates) on a trip to Florida.

*

All our stories are peppered with half-truths and inconsistencies and, like my parents, I, too, am riddled with prejudices and contradictions. All I can offer is what I remember, what I've witnessed and felt, and what I've been told. When it came down to it, I tended to believe my mother's side of things. Maybe it was easier to hold on to her truths and dismiss my father's. It was my mother, after all, who was with me every day, at home and at the hospital. It was my mother who I clung to, who I needed most. It was she I pledged my allegiance and love to, even during those times I would betray her.

A Military Expedition

Friday, December 28, 2018

The day after we brought my mother to see Dr. Akkinepally, I drove Jenny to the Greyhound station in Erie, Pennsylvania, and the hospice people arrived. Jenny had to return to Pittsburgh to start a new tutoring job. This, she hoped, would allow her more time to write than her previous tech job, a job she had quit less than a month earlier. Besides, there wasn't room for all three of us. My mother's apartment was small and cluttered. With the hospice people coming and going, and a hospital bed due to arrive, it would only grow smaller.

My mother hadn't exactly chosen hospice. Dr. Akkinepally had said hospice and palliative care were provided by the same office and provided similar services, with the goal of making my mother comfortable. Palliative care could be offered alongside curative treatment, and hospice was end-of-life care. We had scheduled a follow-up appointment with Dr. Akkinepally for January, in case my mother decided to pursue treatment. My mother would eventually instruct me to cancel that appointment, and in that way the choice would be made.

Not long after I returned from the bus station, Becky and Susan arrived, descending on our lives like a military expedition. Becky was a hospice nurse and Susan a social worker. They interrogated my mother and me with a barrage of questions, questions about my mother's medical history, her sleeping and eating habits. They asked about her smoking, whether she took vitamins, if she drank alcohol. They asked if she was depressed or had a history of depression. They asked about family and friends. Who else could help out? Did my mother have any siblings? How long would I be staying?

After the questioning, Becky and Susan walked us through each stage of cancer and the dying process like two real estate agents walking us through a house we might buy. Palliative care, they told us, was not about curing my mother but improving the quality of the life she had left. It was about comfort and relieving suffering. They asked my mother what her goals were, her expectations.

"I just want to get it over with," my mother said.

Though Becky assured me they were also there for me, I felt overwhelmed and answered questions without fully understanding what I was being asked—or what was being asked of me. Was this how my mother and father felt those first years of my life—with all the uncertainty, the constant upheaval and stress?

Susan read off a checklist: hospital bed, shower chair, medications. Everything would be covered 100%. She suggested, since my mother insisted on staying in her apartment, that we also get an emergency alert bracelet, which would cost $35 per month.

Sherri, the nurse's aide, would arrive the following day and come each day after to make sure my mother took her medications, to give her a shower, wash her hair and rub her with lotion, and do whatever else was needed, even make breakfast if my mother had an appetite. The problem was that she would only be there for an hour a day.

"What about the other twenty-three?" Susan asked. "Who will be with your mother?"

I told them I was planning on driving back to Pittsburgh on Tuesday, as I would soon be out of vacation days (I worked as a front desk clerk at a urology clinic). FMLA—Family Medical Leave Act, unpaid family leave—would help, but I didn't have enough savings to take off work indefinitely.

"I'll be fine," my mother said. "I just want to stay here in my apartment, okay?"

I could tell by the looks on their faces that Susan and Becky were skeptical about the idea of my mother living here by herself.

"I want my mother to come to Pittsburgh," I finally said.

"That's a good idea," Becky replied. "I'm not sure it's safe for you anymore to live alone," she said, turning to my mother.

I told them that's also what Dr. Akkinepally said.

"And it's only going to get more difficult," Susan chimed in. And then my mother began to cry.

I sat across from my mother and watched the tears slide down her face, watched as she wiped them away with the backs of her fists like a child, but I remained in my seat and said nothing. I could feel tears welling in my own eyes, but I tried hard not to let them flow. I was afraid of crying in front of her, of breaking down, of not being able to control myself.

"I'll think about it," my mother whispered.

Sherri

Saturday, December 29 – Sunday, December 30, 2018

Sherri arrived at 11:30 a.m. on Saturday, as I sat watching television, losing myself in the day's headlines. She appeared to be in her mid-fifties. She had poofy 80s hair like the girls I went to high school with. My mother seemed relaxed in her company. I could see the tension in her jaw lessen as she and Sherri made small talk. By the end of that first hour, the two of them had developed a banter, as if they were merely picking up the thread of an earlier conversation, like old friends. It was as if my mother had forgotten why Sherri was there, forgotten she had cancer. They talked about a Dunkirk I barely knew. Names and places ricocheted back and forth. Some were familiar like Catalano, Jaffray, and Ludlum, some were not. *Do you remember so and so? How about that place, oh where was it now, off Lake Shore Drive?*

"Yes," my mother would say, as if the memory had brought back a rush of feelings she'd kept tucked away somewhere deep inside. "I used to go to sock hops there," she said, referring to the pavilion at Wright Park Beach. "That's where I won a jitterbug contest with Gerald."

The following day, I went out to buy groceries. It felt good just to get outside and breathe the fresh air, to go for a drive. When I returned, I found my mother and Sherri looking at all my mother's Elvis and Kennedy memorabilia: an Elvis-in-Hawaii figurine, a statue of JFK in his rocking chair, and a supposed lock of Elvis' hair in a dime bag that my uncle Joe bought on eBay.

"You know, I got to touch Bobby once," my mother

exclaimed, as she showed Sherri a photo of Bobby Kennedy standing next to a painting of Jesus crowned with thorns. "He came to Dunkirk, not long before he was shot. My girlfriend Loretta shoved me right into him."

When Sherri came the next day, my mother suddenly stood up on her own, with only the help of her walker, and went to the bathroom.

"That hydrocodone is a miracle," she announced upon returning, her voice suddenly filled with strength.

I knew then, seeing that hopeful smile that swallowed her face, that my mother had no intention of moving to Pittsburgh.

Crime-Fighting Duo

1979 - 1980

My mother was always the center of my world, my *axis mundi,* and together we were like a crime-fighting duo, speeding around town in our Pontiac 1000, a white, two-door hatchback my grandfather bought after our Bonneville bit the dust in the KFC parking lot. My grandfather would buy every car my mother owned after my parents' separation. And even though we didn't always have enough money for groceries or utility bills, my mother often splurged on what my grandfather referred to as luxuries.

Once, on a whim, she commissioned the guys at Ralph's Garage to paint our names on the doors in blue cursive—her name on the driver's side, mine on the passenger's.

Sometimes we'd jump in the car and my mother would just drive. We'd meander down back roads only to end up at some diner or a thrift store. Sometimes we'd go to the movies, but more often than not, my mother would park outside the theater, and wait in the car while I'd run in and buy a tub of popcorn with extra butter and salt, and we'd go home and watch one of our favorite TV shows: *Dallas*, *Happy Days*, or *The Love Boat*.

My mother never had a boyfriend that I was aware of. She never went on dates or hung out in bars. Instead, evenings found us settled on opposite couches in the living room. Sometimes she'd read one of her paperback novels, crochet an afghan, or fall asleep as the television projected its grainy blue light and I sat with my *Funk & Wagnalls World Atlas*, studying rivers and mountains and oceans, plotting imaginary journeys to far-off places like Los Angeles, Dublin, and New York City.

For dinner we ate Swanson's TV dinners, cube steaks, or my mother's homemade meatloaf, along with a side of canned lima beans, spinach, or asparagus, our favorite, which we slathered with butter and salt.

"Isn't it delicious?" my mother would exclaim, biting into a soggy stalk. It wasn't until I was in my twenties that I realized I could go to the grocery store and buy fresh asparagus, though nothing would ever taste as good as the canned asparagus we shared.

To say that I demanded my mother's undivided attention, that I was a little neurotic, was an understatement. I used to always bite the inside of my cheek when chewing food and would constantly ask her to check to see if I was bleeding. Once, I even burst into the bathroom while she was sitting on the toilet. "Am I bleeding?" I screamed. Without saying a word, my mother leaned forward and examined my mouth.

My mother doted on me because she loved me, but also because of all my health problems. Each morning, she fixed a cheese sandwich for my lunch at school—Miracle Whip on two slices of white bread with the crust cut off and two slices of American cheese in the middle. Sometimes a cheese sandwich was the only food I could keep down. Dr. Jewett, who had repaired my esophagus, told me to chew my food slowly. Some days I'd chew so slowly I'd still be sitting in the cafeteria when my classmates had gone outside for recess, and I'd finish my lunch with the junior high kids.

When my esophagus constricted and I was unable to keep even water down, my mother would drive me to Children's Hospital and Dr. Jewett would dilate my esophagus with a long tube that had a balloon on one end. These constrictions happened at random, without warning, the way my feeding tube popped out when I was a baby. I'd gasp and puke and puke again, and end up in the hospital for days at a time, sometimes weeks.

Despite these hospitalizations, most of the time my mother and I were happy. But one day I found her sitting on our front porch crying. It was summer and we were supposed to go to the beach with my cousin Aiesha and aunt Stephanie.

"What's wrong?" I asked, but my mother waved me away. I ran to my room and sulked, thinking I'd done something to upset her. I could count on one hand the times I had seen her cry: the day Elvis died, the day my father moved out, and the day Mrs. Bankowski, the school librarian, called on the phone and accused my mother of nearly running over her son outside of school. Somehow, this day on the front porch was different, but I couldn't say how or why.

An hour later she stood in the doorway of my room, a smile spread across her face.

"Are you ready?" she asked. "Let's go." She never said what was bothering her. We hopped in our car and headed for the beach. We were a crime-fighting duo, after all. Nothing could defeat us.

Two of Us

December 2018

The week I spent with my mother, after Jenny returned to Pittsburgh, was surreal. It was the most time we had spent in each other's company since I moved away to attend grad school.

The hospice people had devised a regimen for my mother to follow, forcing her to wake up earlier than she was used to. Years of working the night shift, fluctuating thyroid medications, as well as a lifetime of worry, had fostered erratic sleeping patterns. Yes, she looked forward to Sherri's daily visits, which seemed to give her a sense of purpose and hope, but didn't like being told what to do and when to do it. She called it an intrusion. She called it bullshit, but abided as best she could.

When Sherri and the other people from hospice weren't around, we spent our time looking through her scrapbooks, yearbooks, and photo albums, and talked about our lives in ways we never had before.

Under my mother's senior photo in her yearbook, she's described as "a live wire" with a "pleasant personality" and having "a kind word toward all." She was a member of the Latin club and the history league, and was on the yearbook and school newspaper staff. She was known then as "Aud" or "Tiger-Lil," a name given to her by local DJ Boots Bell, who worked at WBUZ in the nearby town of Fredonia.

"Loretta and I used to skip school and walk all the way to the radio station to see Boots," my mother proudly proclaimed. Loretta, or "Lotti," had been my mother's best friend all throughout junior high and high school. They'd lost touch over the years but reconnected through Facebook about a year before Loretta died in 2013.

"I really miss her," my mother said. "We had such fun together. I miss Vinny, too." Vinny was Loretta's kid brother, who was killed in Vietnam.

In one of her scrapbooks, I found a photo taken around Christmas, 1960 or '61. In it, my grandparents, my mother and my uncle Joe pose in front of the tree. My grandfather stands in profile on the far left. He has a wide, mischievous smile and appears to be tickling my grandmother, who is doing her best to keep from laughing and maintain her pose for the camera. The viewer's eyes, however, are immediately drawn to my mother, who stands front and center, leaning forward, as if playfully taunting whoever is taking the photo. She's wearing a green dress, and her dark hair is piled atop her head. My uncle Joe appears solemn, clean shaven like I've never known him, dressed in a dark suit and tie. His hands rest on my mother's shoulders as if he's trying to hold her still or protect her from some unseen danger. Or maybe this was all in my mind.

Other photos show my mother posing with friends from her days in Bethesda and Washington, D.C. In them she looks like some Italian Neorealist starlet, beautiful and alluring, with a "go-ahead-dare-me" smile. There were photos of weddings and parties, and men she dated. There was a friend from India dressed in a yellow sari, another from Ireland, someone who dated James Brown, someone who died in a car accident. During her time there, my mother hung out at a bar owned by one of the Redskins. She even met Vince Lombardi. There were photos from Georgetown, which she talked of often, with a sort of longing and regret. She loved the cobblestone streets and architecture, which dated back to the mid-1700s.

What would her life have been like if she hadn't moved back to Dunkirk? Maybe she'd have married one of the Redskins, or a senator. Maybe her eclectic eye for color and symmetry would have bloomed and she'd have become an artist in her own right, or an interior designer, although her life in Dunkirk was colorful enough. Several pages in her scrapbook were devoted to two of her boyfriends. Both were named Rolph and both had served in the Navy. The glossy 8x10 black-and-white portraits showed them brooding James Dean style. Over the last few years my mother had gotten back in contact with one of them. This Rolph's mother was from Germany and owned a bakery in Dunkirk. My grandfather referred to him as "The Nazi." Rolph and my mother talked on the phone and wrote each other. In his letters, Rolph told my mother about his wife who had died years earlier and of the PTSD he suffered from his time in Vietnam. Once, he surprised my mother by driving his motorcycle all the way from Massachusetts to visit her.

Then there was the singer she was engaged to. "He was from Erie, but I forget his name," my mother admitted, laughing. "He used to sing that song 'Beyond the Sea.'" It was a song made popular by Bobby Darin. When I asked why they didn't get married my mother couldn't remember that either. "Ask your uncle," she said. "He'll know."

*

My mother's phone must have rung twenty times a day, every day, that week, yet mostly she ignored it. "It's just creditors," she scoffed. "And they ain't getting anything from me."

Even when her friend Barb's name and number flashed across the TV screen, she ignored it. "All she does is talk to me about the stupid TV shows she watches," my mother said. She told me how Barb had been struggling with an addiction to painkillers. This led to her recounting the time when she asked my aunt Stephanie to take her to the store to buy a meat and cheese tray after Barb's husband died. Forgetting that she'd had a stroke and lost the use of her left arm, my mother told my aunt that she didn't need help carrying the tray to Barb's front door, where she planned to leave it.

As my mother climbed the stairs she dropped the tray and spilled its contents.

"Meat and cheese went everywhere—on the porch, in the bushes, on the sidewalk, the grass, the tulips," my mother exclaimed with a lilt of glee in her voice, remembering it as if it had just happened. My aunt rushed from the car and the two of them did their best to put all the food back on the tray, picking out the dirt and grass, then left it on the porch and made their getaway.

When my mother started laughing—a series of staccato snorts, which sounded like some strange mix of a brass instrument and wild animal—she would start to choke. You couldn't help but laugh along with her. You couldn't help but choke and gasp and press your hand to your heart.

One night, toward the end of the week, as snow fell outside the sliding glass door, piling up on the balcony, Petula Clark sang from the oldies station, summoning us to forget our troubles and go *Down-towwwwn!* My mother sat on the edge of her hospital bed waiting for me to help her to the bathroom. A spear of moonlight lit the left side of her face, giving her a gaunt, ghostly appearance. The truth was, whether I admitted it to myself or not, my mother was slowly disappearing before my eyes, curling into herself like the edges of the photographs in her scrapbooks. When I took her right arm in mine, I could feel her bones. Within a few days she'd lose her appetite. "Nothing tastes good anymore," she'd say. "I'm just not hungry."

She would also need bigger and bigger doses of hydrocodone, the "miracle drug" as she referred to it, to dull the pain that would soon consume her.

Blaze of Glory

1980

Music could always be heard in our house. Before the oldies station on my mother's cable TV, there were records (LPs and 45s) that my parents listened to. We had a small turntable that looked like a suitcase and had a prominent spot on the wall-length bookshelf in my father's study. He even ran wires through the drop-ceilings and put a speaker in the bathroom so my mother could listen to music while she took a shower.

I remember sitting on the floor watching my parents dance to Chubby Checker's "The Twist," their bodies bending and gyrating as Checker called out *Round and round and up and down we go* like a shaman, beckoning them to partake in this ritual of body and soul, while Joe Macho's bass kept the beat and Georgie Young burped arpeggios on the sax.

After my father moved out, my mother transformed his study into a music room. Gone were his roll-top desk, his commemorative plate from Oral Roberts, as well as a framed picture of a chimp dressed in a three-piece suit. Gone were his stock charts that looked like EKG readings, his lottery magazines and thick tomes on economics—all of which he studied like scripture. In their place, my mother dragged the tattered yellow loveseat from the living room. She hung a poster of Elvis and a painting of Jesus exposing his sacred heart. She opened the curtains, hung spider plants and ferns in the bay window, and sprayed something that smelled like the lilac tree in our backyard.

During this time, it had become my job to wake my mother each morning so she could help me get ready for school. Her clock/radio went off at 7:15 a.m. and I'd hobble into her bedroom. The clock was just a few inches from her head on her nightstand, but it might as well have been down the street, for she never heard it. "Mom, it's time to get up!" I'd shout.

"Five more minutes," she'd beg, her eyes momentarily springing open. Then she'd turn over, pull the covers over her head, and groan. "Please, just give me five more minutes."

I'd press the snooze button, run into the kitchen, turn on the Mr. Coffee maker and then make her toast slathered with butter and powdered cinnamon.

One December morning, I hobbled into my mother's bedroom and called her as usual. Instead of pressing the snooze button, I stood and listened to the radio announcer, who sounded as if he'd been crying. "John Lennon was assassinated outside his apartment in New York City last night," he said. "He was forty years old."

I had no idea who this guy Lennon was, but the word "assassinated" filled me with a mix of fear and excitement. It sounded so adult, so cool. All that day and for the next few weeks, the radio and TV were abuzz about him and his former band The Beatles.

A week later, my cousin Aiesha and I watched the televised memorial service. Thousands of people had gathered outside The Dakota. They stood crying and singing Lennon's songs "Give Peace a Chance" and "Imagine."

I soon became obsessed with everything Lennon, including the gory details of his murder, the same way I was obsessed, a few years earlier, with the film *The Lincoln Conspiracy.* I had begged my mother to take me to the theater, just to see Lincoln's brains fly out of his head. Now, my attention turned to Mark David Chapman, a Beatles fan who flew all the way from Hawaii just to shoot Lennon, and the two bullets that struck the left side of Lennon's back. One lodged in his aorta, destroying the major blood vessels above his heart on impact.

I often fantasized about being assassinated. Sometimes, in the privacy of my room, or standing in front of the bathroom mirror, I spoke in a reporter's voice and narrated the bloody scene: *Irwin was found riddled with bullets* or *The killer attacked Irwin with a hatchet.*

Was I psychotic? Was my obsession with being murdered some kind of internalized martyr complex that I learned from my mother? Did it foreshadow, along with my magic marker drawings of Jesus being crucified, or the G.I. Joe figures that I carved up and set on fire, some predilection to violence? Or was I no different from other boys my age who'd fallen in love with death, or at least the idea of it?

Even though I couldn't articulate how, I knew that Lennon's death changed everything. After I found a copy of The Beatles' *Revolver* hidden among my mother's Elvis and Barry Manilow records, I listened to it constantly. It was as if I'd been reborn and my destiny revealed. I no longer wanted to be a firefighter, the quarterback for the Buffalo Bills, or Rocky Balboa. I'd be a rock star one day and go down in a blaze of glory. Why else had I been born? Why else had I survived so many hospitalizations and surgeries?

Small Tragedies

December 2018

"It is not our job to remain unbroken," wrote poet Robert Bly in "A Home in Dark Grass." "Our task is to lose our leaves and be born again." This was a truth my mother had always understood. She also knew, partly from experience, that life was filled with small tragedies that happen every day, and the many ways these tragedies could undermine a person and send them reeling into a vicious cycle of despair.

"Always be kind," she'd tell me. "There's always someone worse off than you."

My mother accepted people for who and what they were, with all their faults and vices, their contradictions and cruelties. She possessed a disarming aura that made people feel at ease, made them feel as if they were important. These people were drawn to my mother, people like my best friend JoJo, and our neighbor Ronnie, who found the effort it took to navigate through life nearly impossible.

I remember Ronnie sitting on our living room floor one night, knees pressed against his chest, his hands covering his face, as he sobbed. He told my mother he felt useless since the steel mill where he'd worked had closed. He said he felt angry, unhinged. He couldn't stop drinking. He said alcohol was the only thing that got him through. He said he was ashamed of what he was putting his wife and daughters through. He said he was scared, but he didn't have the courage to change.

I don't remember what my mother said to Ronnie, but I know that he suffered for a long time. Eventually, he pulled himself together, quit drinking, and found another job. The last time my mother saw him, he told her he'd been sober for over twenty-five years.

JoJo was the new kid in Ms. Clemens' first grade class when we met. We were inseparable from then on. People who knew us often mistook us for brothers. We were troublemakers and pranksters, always egging the other on. We joined and got thrown out of Cub Scouts together (our mothers were both den mothers), we played football and basketball together, walked to school and rode our bikes together all over town.

It was JoJo who always encouraged me, running alongside me in gym class, humming the theme from *Rocky* as the other kids passed us by. He was also very protective, threatening to kill anyone who made fun of my brace, the way I walked, or questioned why, at age twelve, my bicycle still had training wheels. It was with JoJo that I first drank hard liquor and smoked marijuana. Only three months my senior, he seemed years older, like a big brother, possessing a worldliness and sense of confidence I envied.

There were the nights when he banged on our kitchen door, wanting to use the phone to call around to different clubs and bars in search of his parents. My mother would wake me saying "JoJo's here," and I'd stumble into the kitchen to find him—a phantom plucked from the darkness. My mother warmed a pan of milk on the stove and made us hot chocolate as he'd dial the various phone numbers, all of them memorized, until he found his parents. Then, the three of us sat at the kitchen table drinking our hot chocolate, waiting to hear the car horn that would propel him back into the darkness from where he'd come.

When we were in eighth grade, our mothers took us to see an endocrinologist because we were not growing, compared to the other boys in our class, and neither of us was going through puberty. In the end, JoJo agreed to a series of hormone injections, while I refused.

Nights when we were fourteen or fifteen, we'd sit in his bedroom passing a bottle of Puerto Rican rum, talking about girls and sports, and planning our futures, promising to always remain best friends. But by our sophomore year we began to drift apart. Then, the summer after I graduated from high school, when I was preparing for community college, JoJo was arrested in Oklahoma on a cross-country burglary spree. The last time we saw each other was the day after Christmas 2015, when I visited him in prison. He'd just begun serving a four-to-six-year sentence for possession and sale of crack cocaine.

I wonder if he ever thinks about those late nights he came to my house and my mother made us hot chocolate. I wonder if the problems he faced as an adult had anything to do with the hormone shots he received as a young teenager, or being left to his own devices too often. Or maybe it was just genetics, luck of the draw.

"I still feel sorry for JoJo," my mother said, as we sat waiting for Sherri to arrive. "He was really a good kid at heart."

*

Along with family and friends, strangers also gravitated toward my mother, like the woman who delivered the *Penny Saver.* She cried about her two sons, both of whom were in prison. The guy from the Rent-A-Center, who delivered a sleeper-sofa, told my mother about his chronic back pain and his marriage troubles.

Yet, when she felt threatened or hurt, she often retreated

behind her own protective wall. To her, the slightest infraction felt like a betrayal. She always forgave, but rarely forgot. Like my grandfather and uncle Joe, she had a talent for holding onto decades-old grudges, especially against people who failed to send a sympathy card or attend a wake.

Whenever I did something that hurt my mother, or violated the trust we shared, like lying about where I was going after school, or telling her I didn't love her, or that I loved my childhood friend Robert Lemanski's mother more than her, she wouldn't yell or send me to my room. Those times I felt an overwhelming compulsion to tell her the weird thoughts that filled my pre-teen head—from images of a nude Nastassja Kinski in *Cat People* (a movie, strangely enough, I watched with my mother and my first grade teacher, Miss Clemens) to scenes from the news of war-torn amputated limbs—she wouldn't berate me or frown in disgust.

Instead, she'd employ one of her silent treatments. These stretches of silence could last an entire day. They were so painful to endure that I sometimes wished she'd just beat me the way the Mekus kids, who lived next door, were routinely beaten by their parents. It felt as if I'd been cast into limbo, sentenced to live out the remainder of my days like a ghost. I was always the first to break down, to do or say something I thought would make her laugh or at least acknowledge my presence. I tried to plead for forgiveness, though nothing I said or did swayed her. She'd talk when she was good and ready. Afterward, when I was forgiven and we were friends again, my mother and I picked up where we'd left off. It was as if no time had passed, as if nothing had come between us.

*

Sitting in her apartment that week in late December, the two of us drinking coffee and talking, felt like it did before I moved away. As Dion sang from the oldies station, *Has anybody here seen my old friend John?* I thought about how much of my mother's life I still didn't know—her dreams and disappointments, what gave her the most joy. There was so much I'd never asked her. Where was she when John Kennedy was shot? Did she watch the moon landing on television? Why didn't she ever remarry? Yet somehow, it didn't feel right asking.

New Year's Eve

Monday, December 31, 2018

It had been four days since Dr. Akkinepally confirmed what the emergency room doctor proclaimed: "You have cancer." It was New Year's Eve. Shards of sunlight painted the wall above my mother's bed. I woke around 8 a.m. and lay on the couch watching her sleep. The hydrocodone, besides relieving her pain, helped my mother sleep through the night. Did she dream? I don't know, but she didn't wake me with her nightmare screams, like she did so many times when I was a child.

"No! Stop! Get Away!" she'd cry, and I'd rush to her bedside, shake her and beg her to wake. Who were her nightmares about? Why was she so afraid? Whenever I'd asked, she'd claim she couldn't remember. These nightmares didn't happen every night, but often enough that I became used to them and learned to stay in my bed, pulling the covers over my head until her screaming stopped.

Now, I counted her shallow breaths and the rise and fall of her chest. Sherri was due to arrive by noon. I scanned the room as if to memorize its intricacies. My gaze stopped on a photo of my grandfather on the shelf below the television. In it, he's sitting on the back porch of our house on Fifth Street, his glasses tucked in the breast pocket of a blue bowling shirt. On another shelf sat a photo of my mother posing with her friends Jackie, Barb, and Marlene during happier times—"The Golden Girls," they called themselves.

When my mother finally woke, I brought her pills with orange juice to wash them down, and a cup of coffee. We sat awhile, quietly—each lost in our own thoughts.

When Sherri arrived, she walked my mother into the bathroom for a shower, to shampoo her hair and rub lotion into her sagging skin.

Twenty minutes passed before they returned. "Doesn't she look beautiful?" Sherri asked. "Like a new woman!"

My mother giggled with embarrassment and pride. "I feel great," she exclaimed. "I really feel good."

After Sherri left, my mother and I watched two of her favorite movies. First, *La Bamba*. She cried during the scene where Ritchie Valens' brother hears on the radio about the plane crash that killed Ritchie, Buddy Holly, and The Big Bopper. She cried every time, as if it reminded her of some private grief she still hung on to. Later, we put on *Misery*. The scene where Kathy Bates smashes James Caan's ankles with a hammer made my mother screech with laughter and feign disbelief, as if it were the first time she'd seen it.

After *Misery*, my mother turned on the oldies station. The sounds of The Temptations, Simon & Garfunkel, and Leslie Gore filled the apartment. All the lights, save the one from the television, were turned off—our reflections beaming back at us through the sliding glass door.

"I'm sorry I spoiled Christmas," my mother suddenly said. "I'm sorry I have cancer."

She told me how much she still missed my grandfather, especially at Christmastime, when he'd come over after church.

"I miss him, too," I replied and remembered all those summer days I'd spent with him, playing catch on the sidewalk in front of his house, riding in his car, sitting with him in his green armchair, watching the Yankees on television.

My mother claimed she saw my grandfather after he died,

just as she claimed to have seen the ghost of her mother's mother pass by the living room window when she was a child. Sometimes she caught a whiff of the tobacco my grandfather filled his pipe with.

"He was more of a father to you than your own father," she said. And it was true. As a child I'd spend every other weekend with my father and an hour or so on Thursday evenings, but my grandfather filled in the time in between. It was he who I followed, clumsy as a puppy. It was my grandfather who I looked to when I was trying to figure out what it meant to be a man. What would he have said if he were sitting with us now, I wondered.

"What are you gonna do when I'm not around anymore?" he'd always demand, whenever my mother sent me to his house to ask for money or groceries. "Who you gonna ask then?" Yet in the end he always gave in, telling me he'd write it all down in his little book, and that one day he'd come to collect.

Tomorrow I'd drive back to Pittsburgh, to my job, to Jenny and our life together. What would my grandfather say, knowing I'd be leaving my mother to the care of strangers?

My Grandfather's Pontiac

1980-1985

What did I really know about my grandfather, that mustachioed, pipe-smoking old man who drove me to school each morning? His car horn sounded like cannon fire, shaking the chestnut and maple trees along Main Street. I'd hurry to find my book bag and get out the door while my mother sat at the kitchen table drinking coffee, or snoozing.

As I climbed into the passenger seat of my grandfather's Pontiac, I grew dizzy from the dashboard lights, the intoxicating earthy aroma that emanated from the pipe he was constantly puffing on, and that "new car smell" that never seemed to disappear. In fact, the car always glistened, as if it had just been washed and polished. He always made sure to have the radio set to my favorite station, Buffalo's *97 Rock,* as he piloted me to school or around town—to the grocery store, the pharmacy, or the Buffalo Bills' training camp at Fredonia State College.

When my nana was alive, the three of us drove to Cleveland to visit my uncle Paul and aunt Angie and see the Indians play the Yankees. One time I saw Reggie Jackson hit three homers, but the Yankees still lost. On another occasion, my grandfather drove three hours to a discount clothing store in Pennsylvania. He stood at the counter and pointed to shirts and pants and even shoes he wanted, barking the size he needed to the cashier. Then, he paid and left with his loot, without ever trying anything on. After he died, we found button-down shirts still wrapped in plastic, as well as dozens of packages of white socks shoved in a drawer. "White socks," he used to tell me, to my confusion, "are good for the eyes, for seeing in the dark."

Larry Spacc's garage was another place I enjoyed accompanying my grandfather. At Larry Spacc's he was a legend. All the mechanics and car washers would put down their wrenches and sponges when he arrived, in preparation for what was about to take place. Even Larry himself seemed to have a soft spot for my grandfather hidden beneath the lapel of his three-piece suit.

"You gotta Jew 'em down," my grandfather would instruct me. "Never take the asking price." What Jews? I wondered. The only Jews I knew were the ones in the Bible.

As I stood in my grandfather's slumped shadow, I bore witness to his prodigious negotiating skills. It was pure theatre.

For his part, Larry mumbled and nodded his bulbous head with an air of quiet confidence like the Godfather. Sometimes he'd cast his gaze in my direction and wink, as if to say, "Look at this guy, would ya? He knows he's gonna get the short end of the stick, but he's still fightin'." It was as if he was saying, "You should be proud, kid. You got a hell of a grandpa there."

Even though he threatened to buy a Buick or Oldsmobile, or his dream car, a Cadillac, my grandfather only ever owned Pontiacs and bought them exclusively from Larry Spacc. Larry was Italian after all, and Italians had to stick together, didn't they? Or maybe that's what I imagined I heard Old Man Spacc whisper in my grandfather's ear.

*

Some mornings, when I climbed into my grandfather's car, he'd say "Buongiorno!" But, when I'd ask him to say something else in Italian, he'd claim he only spoke English. English was the language in America, he'd tell me. English was how you got ahead in the world.

My mother, however, contradicted these claims, telling me about the loud arguments my grandfather had with his own father, Giuseppe, in Italian. A shoemaker by trade, Giuseppe immigrated from a small village in Calabria in the first decade of the twentieth century. From New York City, he found his way to the cabbage farms of western New York, where he labored and met his future wife, Jennie Nocito, my great-grandmother, who was fresh from Palermo. Neither of them ever learned more than a handful of words in English.

My grandfather was named Michele, but it was changed to Michael when he started school, just as his surname was Americanized to Rhoda, from its original Rodà. Was he embarrassed of his parents' old world ways, or the fact that they couldn't speak English? Either way, my grandfather would follow a different course than Giuseppe. In 1933, at the height of the depression, long before he met my nana, or began his career in the steel mills, my grandfather put his dreams of studying law on hold and joined FDR's Civilian Conservation Corps. He was just nineteen years old that summer when he traveled, along with thousands of other young men, to the wilds of Idaho, where he helped build roads and bridges and bathed in a river full of snakes. After he died, we found an envelope in a cigar box on the cellar stairs full of postcards he'd written to his parents and his two sisters, Josephine and Antonette. There were photos as well, one of him looking like Woody Guthrie, standing on a rocky bluff, his hands shoved in his pants pockets. In another photo, he sits on a park bench next to a droopy-eyed blonde-haired woman who wore a banded cloche hat with a flower on the side. His sweetheart? A lover? We'd never know.

*

In my early twenties, up until his death, my grandfather and I would go to the Knights of Columbus on Fridays for fish and beer. Afterward, he'd hand me the car keys and instruct me to take him for a ride.

With my grandfather in the passenger seat, I'd propel us down side streets, turning left, then right, then left again all to his nervous amusement. Along the way, he'd point to places that once held significance for him—a bowling alley, a shoe store, the empty lot where my aunt Rose and uncle Neff's house and grocery store used to be, or the senior citizens' center where Holy Trinity Church once stood, where he and my nana were married.

Someday, I thought, as I turned another corner and squinted into the setting sun, no one will be alive to tell these stories, to remember these places and names.

Weekends with My Father

1979-1981

It's true, my father was not around every day like my grandfather, but I enjoyed the time we spent together during those first few years after he and my mother separated. On Thursdays, he'd bring my mother the $50 in child support he was ordered to pay, always in cash. He'd set it on the counter next to the toaster and stand awkwardly for a moment. I can still picture him, how small he appeared, unsure of what to say or do, as my mother sat at the table smoking a cigarette. After a few minutes of small talk, I'd follow my father out the door and he'd take me to dinner, and sometimes, if he were in a good mood, to the movies. Mostly, he'd have me back home within the hour. If you'd asked my mother, however, she'd scoff and tell you that my memory of those years was skewed, that my father's presence in my life was mostly nonexistent.

On those weekends I stayed with my father, he'd pick me up in his rusted Chevy Nova. He'd drive west on Route 5 toward Barcelona and my grandmother's house, one hand on the wheel, the other resting in his crotch, while I looked out the window at the passing trees, and the clouds, thankful for the silence, for not feeling the pressure to talk. Yet, sometimes this silence filled me with anxiety. My father kept a club under the front seat—three steel rods wrapped in rubber. He liked showing off the one-inch gash in the rubber, where he claimed he'd hit someone when he was younger. He also kept a Dirty Harry style gun under the floor mats. He had a reputation when he was younger, my mother told me, as a fighter. Sometimes it seemed like he wanted something to happen, to justify using them.

Before arriving at my grandmother's house, we'd stop at the dock to watch the seagulls and boats on the lake. On a hill overlooking the dock stood a stone lighthouse, the first gas-powered lighthouse in the world. The small caretaker's cottage that sat beside it was where my father was born.

At my grandmother's house, my father and I would set up camp in the living room while my grandmother stayed in the kitchen to give my father and me our court-appointed "quality time." When she'd come to check up on us, she'd often find us mooing like cows or quacking like ducks. My excitement at spending the weekend with my father often wore off, however, and I'd hide in the bathroom, staring at my reflection in the mirror, trying to find some resemblance to him—an eyebrow, an expression, or curl of the lip. Maybe I was just too sensitive. I wondered if he knew that, even though I loved him, I desperately missed my mother. Did he know that whenever he gave me money—for Christmas, or on my birthday—I'd give it to her when I got home? Despite the camaraderie that seemed to flourish during those early years, I always felt a distance between us, an unease.

"What's new?" my father would ask.

"Not much," I'd reply.

As I grew older, it became our script, like our very own sitcom. Our conversations were brief and sometimes painful, populated by long silences. I learned to predict his responses. If I had some news, or something important to tell him, he'd nod his head, say, "Oh yeah?" then change the subject. Then we'd turn to the television to relieve us of the burden of talking. Television became our mediator, as I'm sure it did in households across the country.

This is not to say that my father never showed affection, that he didn't indulge me, or try to make a show of his love with yearly trips to Niagara Falls, the county fair, or some amusement park. He often showered me with expensive Christmas and birthday presents, and he tried to do some traditional father-son activities. He hung a netless basketball hoop on a pole near the garage for shooting hoops, for example, and bought me a bow and arrow and taught me how to hit a bullseye.

I still have the black-and-white photographs he took with his Instamatic camera of me pretending to be Clark Kent and/or Superman. In the first photograph, I'm posing in a pair of sunglasses and my clip-on Catholic school tie, my hands thrust into the pockets of my plaid pants. In the second, I'm pressed against the faux wood-paneled walls of our dining room in a small phone-booth-sized space between the china cabinet and the corner, where I ripped my button-down shirt open to reveal a Superman T-shirt underneath. In the third photograph, I'm wearing a bath towel cape and showing off my Man-of-Steel strength by lifting a chair in the living room. In the fourth, I'm lying on the floor with a woeful expression, next to my father's glass paperweight, which I pretended was Kryptonite.

It was my grandmother, however, Ruth Estelle Irwin, who made these visits not only tolerable, but fun. Whenever my father and I grew weary of each other or ran out of things to talk about, or if he went off on one of his tangents about the government or what he'd buy when he won the lottery, I'd tiptoe into the kitchen, where my grandmother sat playing solitaire or watching her own TV shows on a small black-and-white set in the corner of the table.

Like my nana, my grandma Irwin doted on me. She made me fried Spam sandwiches, homemade bread and butter pickles, and deviled eggs, pushed her false teeth out with her tongue to make me laugh, and marked my growth with pencil slashes on the kitchen doorframe. Unlike my nana, however, my grandma Irwin was adventurous and worldly. She had a degree from a business college and worked at a bank, and after retirement she traveled around the country with fellow seniors on bus trips, mailing me postcards from the Badlands, Nova Scotia, and Branson, Missouri. Besides sewing, knitting, and crocheting, she enjoyed country music, romance novels, and listening to her police scanner, which she kept set to the maximum volume, much to my father's annoyance.

Sometimes, she'd set a dusty photo album in front of me. As we turned the pages, she'd tell me stories about the people in the photographs—soldiers, fishermen, farmers, Grange members, Pilgrims—people like Doc Isham, my great-great-grandfather, who had his foot shot off in the Battle of Chancellorsville. These people came from places like Glastonbury, County Down, Plymouth.

It was in these pages that I first saw photographs of my grandfather, Edwin Hartwell Irwin, though most of his life remained a mystery. I knew he and my grandmother were married on Christmas Day in 1935. They had two sons, my father and his older brother Edwin Jr. (Bud). I knew he was a member of the Loyal Order of Moose and the Grange, and that he worked as a farmer, steel worker, fisherman, and general laborer. I knew that he died in 1964, at age fifty-three, from a cerebral hemorrhage. My grandmother, father, and uncle all said it was the result of a beating he suffered a few years prior, though neither could remember exactly when the beating happened.

At the time—1960 or '61—my grandfather and father were living together in Niagara Falls and working construction, building the Robert Moses Hydroelectric Power Station. When it opened in 1961, it was the largest hydroelectric plant in the Western world.

According to my grandmother, my grandfather had a few days off one weekend and drove from Lewiston to Westfield (about 90 miles) to see her. My father had to work and stayed behind. On my grandfather's return trip to Lewiston, he took an alternate route and ended up in a bad neighborhood in downtown Buffalo. Even at fifteen I knew that when she said "bad neighborhood" she meant a Black neighborhood.

In this "bad neighborhood," my grandfather's car stalled. He got out of the car, lifted the hood, and was assaulted by three Black men who beat him, kicked him in the head, and left him for dead.

Somehow, my grandfather found the strength to stand, and when he tried the engine again, it started just as mysteriously as it had stalled. Then he drove in search of a hospital, only to be hit by another car that had run a red light. Like a scene from a movie, a taxi appeared, but the driver, seeing the shape my grandfather was in, all the blood, refused to give him a ride. Finally, a police officer arrived on the scene and drove my grandfather to a hospital, where he underwent emergency brain surgery.

"His head was all bandaged," my grandmother said. "They had him in a tub of ice to bring the swelling down. He lost the sight in one eye and never really recovered."

The story of my grandfather's beating and death took on mythic proportions in my mind. As I grew older, however, I began to question the details, which were murky to begin with, and changed, depending on who was retelling the story. This questioning was all in my head. I found it impossible to admit my doubts to my father, grandmother, or uncle.

"If I'd been there that day," my father said, on those rare occasions he'd speak of the incident, "I'd a shot all them Black bastards."

I cringed. I never once heard my mother use racial slurs or talk disparagingly about Blacks, or Puerto Ricans (who made up a notable percentage of the local population), so I was shocked when my father talked about them in a derogatory way.

Sometimes I think he wished he were with my grandfather the day he was beaten, just so he could prove his worth, like all those action movies he loved, starring Charles Bronson, Clint Eastwood, or Bruce Willis, where the hero's loved ones are murdered, and he takes revenge on the killers. My father always seemed ready for a fight, to right some wrong—real or imaginary.

Of all the stories he's told about his youth, his favorite was about how he overcame being bullied as a child. He was overweight. Other kids called him *Fat Boy Irwin* and beat him up. In high school, he started lifting weights and exercising at an obsessive rate—a thousand push-ups a day, he once told me. By the end of his senior year, he'd lost a hundred pounds and transformed his body into a lean, muscular fighting machine.

"I went around and whooped 'em all," my father often boasted, flexing his biceps, and together we laughed, basking in that long-ago triumph.

Stations of the Cross

1978 – 1981

When my father was still a part of our daily lives, he, my mother, and I went to Saturday evening Mass at Saint Elizabeth's. Then sometimes on Thursdays, we'd attend a service in the basement of a church in Silver Creek, a town ten miles east of Dunkirk. There, my father waited in line with other parishioners while my mother and I stayed in our seats. The minister stood on the altar and shouted as each person in line stood before him. Then, he slapped them on the forehead, causing them to fall backward into the arms of the person behind them. When my father fell, I leaped from my seat, frightened he'd been hurt, though my mother reassured me he was okay. She said he'd been "slain in the Spirit."

On Sunday mornings, I held my father's hand as he knelt in front of our television and prayed along with Oral Roberts, who told us we should expect a miracle. My mother told me my father prayed for my health and for him to become a millionaire. My health did improve, but my father, to the best of my knowledge, never became a millionaire.

Not long after my father moved out, my mother joined a folk choir at Saint Elizabeth's, led by Sam Mancuso and his wife, Joanne. Suddenly, instead of Elvis, Willie Nelson, Air Supply, and Queen, my mother started listening to what she called Christian folk music—men and women with acoustic guitars, tambourines, and flutes who sang songs praising Jesus.

*

Saturday was house-cleaning day. With a lit cigarette dangling between her lips, my mother moved from room to room, dusting, polishing, vacuuming, mopping, and spraying air freshener. When she didn't have a cigarette in her mouth, she sang along in her exuberantly off-key voice to the music that seemed to emanate from every room. My mother's new musical heroes included John Michael Talbot—a monk who played classical guitar, a band called Earthen Vessels, and Reverend Carey Landry, whose song "Bring Me A Rose" I embarrassingly sang along to. It was *Jesus Christ Superstar,* however, that my mother played most often and loudest.

Everything's alright! my mother sang along with Yvonne Elliman—who played Mary Magdalene on the original studio recording. *Everything's alright, yes, everything's fine*, she sang, even when it wasn't—even when she had to go to my grandparents for money to buy groceries or pay the gas bill. It became her new mantra.

When my mother sang along with "I Don't Know How to Love Him," she became enraptured. Her eyes glazed with a faraway dreamy look, her voice tinged with a desperate mournfulness. *Should I bring him down? Should I scream and shout? Should I speak of love? Let my feelings out?* Did she see herself as Mary Magdalene—the woman who anointed Jesus' feet with oil after he freed her from seven devils?

Around this time, my mother and I started attending 7:00 p.m. Mass at Saint Elizabeth's every weeknight. I loved 7:00 p.m. Mass—the organ music, the prayers, the candles. I liked dropping a dollar in the collection basket, and the way Father Menge tilted his head like a bird as he read from the Gospels. I liked Father Doyle's long curly hair and glasses, which made him look like John Lennon. Most of all, I loved the Stations of the Cross, which were performed on Thursdays during Lent. They celebrated Christ's passion, beginning when Jesus was arrested in Gethsemane, and moved on to his trial before Pilate, his march toward Golgotha, and then his crucifixion. As the Stations were performed, the priest and altar boys stopped at each of the fourteen Stations, where prayers and blessings were recited. My mother and I always sat on the far right, about halfway up the aisle below the 11th Station, which depicted a Roman soldier pounding nails into Jesus' hands and feet. It was my favorite Station.

I also became transfixed by the life-sized plaster crucifix that hung on the far wall near the door to the choir room. Sometimes, I imagined it was made of white chocolate, like the Cadbury bunnies my nana gave me for Easter. Sometimes it was the skull of some prehistoric longhorn, or a kite, sailing across the sky. In my mind, I pictured the blood flowing like tiny rivers down Jesus' body.

Besides my mother and me, there were a dozen or so other regulars in attendance. Front and center were three old ladies who, each evening, arrived an hour early to recite the rosary together. They remained on their knees throughout the Mass, moaning and shifting their hulking bodies as if one, like a mountain range seized by seismic tremors. My mother told me they were all in love with Father Menge, who bore a striking resemblance to Cary Grant with his salt-and-pepper hair and horn-rimmed glasses.

In the center aisle, along with his parents, sat Rocky. Rocky was in his mid-twenties, maybe thirty. He had black curly hair and a mouth that seemed perpetually ajar. My mother said he was retarded, but insisted I not use that word. Rocky's mother was a cook at a local soup kitchen and his father was a deacon for the Saturday morning Spanish services.

Rocky always had two superhero action figures with him. He held one in each hand—Spiderman and Aquaman, or Captain America and the Hulk. He would reach up and place them atop his father's head, where they'd battle it out in a fist-flying, leg-spinning duel to the death. When his father had had enough, he motioned for Rocky to stop, which caused Rocky to assault him with kisses—rapid pecks to his face and head. There was something about Rocky I envied, even though he had intellectual disabilities. Maybe it was his sense of innocence, or the affection his father so easily showed him.

As my mother stood mouthing The Apostles' Creed—*I believe in God the Father almighty, creator of heaven and earth*—my mind wandered, and my eyes once again fell on the giant crucifix. I imagined the drawings I'd create at home when Mass was over—magic marker portraits of Jesus looking like Father Doyle, or John Lennon on the cover of *Abbey Road,* with scarlet red blood pouring from his head, fists, feet, and side. Sometimes, I imagined myself dead. In my mind I could see the sorrowful expression on my mother's face as she—the way Mary cradled Jesus in the 13th Station—held my corpse in her arms.

New Year's Day

Tuesday, January 1, 2019

While my mother slept, I read T.S. Eliot's *Four Quartets*. "In my beginning is my end," he writes in the "East Coker" section. Had my mother and I arrived at such a place?

When my mother woke, I noticed how much her appearance had transformed overnight. Her eyes, which betrayed a mix of bewilderment and fear, looked large and woeful. It made me think of when I visited my cousin Phil in 2015. He was in the hospital in New Jersey, suffering from leukemia. At the time, I'd not seen him or his wife Geraldine in many years, and the sight of him—his eyes large and watery, nearly filling his whole face, and his body so small and withered—shocked me so much I couldn't speak, yet I couldn't turn away either. He told me that when he got better, he wanted to come to Pittsburgh and that he looked forward to meeting Jenny. He died four months later.

After I gave my mother her pills and poured us both a cup of coffee, I packed my clothes and my frayed copy of *Four Quartets* in my duffel bag. Once Sherri arrived, I kissed my mother on the head, gathered my stuff, and closed her apartment door behind me. Outside, I put my car in drive and pulled out of the parking lot. In my mind I could hear the emergency room doctor's voice repeating, "You have cancer. You have cancer" as well as my grandfather's, and his accusatory question, "What are you gonna do when I'm gone?"

My mother told the hospice people that she just wanted to get it over with. *It,* meaning the business of dying. Her life. Is that what I wanted, too, to get it over with? To get past it? To move on? My plan was to come back in two days. Surely, she'd be okay for two days. Yet, I knew if the tables were turned, my mother would never have left me to the care of strangers. As I pondered this, I felt the desire to just drive away and never return, just keep driving until either the gas or the road ran out, driving as if I could escape.

Life-Changing Surgery

1981

On Father's Day, four weeks before my tenth birthday, my mother and I flew to Baltimore. It was only the second time I'd flown on a plane. A year earlier, we took one to visit Gerald and celebrate his 40th birthday. At that time, when the plane began to climb into the sky, I stood up and screamed "I'm having a heart attack!"

Now, I was scheduled to have major surgery at Johns Hopkins. The main question, however, was whether my bladder would work. Was there too much nerve damage, as earlier tests had shown? Would signals from my brain reach my bladder? I had never felt the sensation of having to pee before. If the surgery went as planned, I'd have to be potty-trained like a toddler. It was a huge moment in my mother's life and my life.

Father Richard Burke, a priest, and brother of one of my mother's best friends, Margaret, picked us up at the airport. Father Burke was studying canon law in Washington, D.C., and was often summoned to the Vatican by Pope John Paul II, who just a month earlier had been shot by a Turkish assassin. Three years later, Margaret, nine months pregnant with her fifth child, would die in a car crash.

Dr. Engel's plan was to close my ileostomy—the two tiny holes Dr. Dwoskin drilled into my right side the day I was born. They were a direct line to my double kidney. Dr. Engel would attempt to reroute my ureters to my bladder. We all hoped that I'd be able to pee from my penis and would no longer have to wear diapers.

In the days leading up to my surgery, I underwent another round of tests. Dr. Engel concluded that his original plan would not work. Plan B was nearly as complex and risky. Dr. Engel would remove my neurogenic bladder and create a stoma on the right side of my abdomen. I would have to wear a second bag, but, if everything went well, I'd be free of diapers.

From the window of my room at the far end of the hallway on the children's floor, I could see the baseball stadium where the Orioles played. The nurses provided my mother with a cot, pillows and blankets. When I wasn't having tests, I explored the hospital's maze of buildings. A favorite place, besides the cafeteria, was the Billings Administration Building, with its massive rotunda and 10½ foot marble statue of "Christus Consoler," or "The Divine Healer," whose outstretched arms welcomed all who passed.

Back on the children's floor, I spent my afternoons in the game room, across the hall from the nurses' station, drawing and playing with the robot phone booth. It was there I met kids from Texas, Poland, and Peking, yellow kids and Black kids, kids with cystic fibrosis and cancer and bulging eyes, kids, who like me, had traveled to Hopkins with the hopes that the doctors and nurses would work miracles in their lives. There was a girl from Tel Aviv who had a tumor the size of a grapefruit growing out of the side of her face and a five-year-old Black girl who had two prosthetic legs.

Two days before my surgery, my grandpa and nana arrived. My father came the next day. I stood in the doorway of my room waiting for him. Finally, in the late afternoon, the unit door opened, and my father walked through. He looked taller than I'd remembered. He'd even shaved his Magnum P.I. mustache.

"Dad!" I screamed, and raced down the hallway as fast as

my crippled body would allow, the cork lift of my brace thumping on the tiled floor with each step, until I flew into his outstretched arms. For a moment he, held me suspended in the air above him, our foreheads touching, our faces stretched into goofy smiles.

The following morning, I was wheeled down to the operating room. My mother, father, and grandparents gathered around the gurney where I lay, wrapped in a warm blanket. Each kissed me and told me they would see me when the surgery was over.

On the operating table, shadows like giant birds hovered above me. A pair of hands placed a rubber mask that smelled like epoxy and made me nauseous over my face. Then, a voice called out and instructed me to count backward from one hundred. By the time I got to ninety-eight, the table started to spin like a roulette wheel, and the lights above me—huge insect eyes—shone brighter than the sun. I felt as if they were pulling me closer, reeling me in. Then, everything went black, and I was lost in that familiar void, falling like Icarus, falling, and falling without end.

The next thing I remembered, I was in the bed in my hospital room with an IV in my left arm and a nasogastric (NG) tube down my nose. My grandfather sat in a chair to my right. He held my hand, and whistled softly, as he often did when he was nervous. My surgery, though successful, had lasted thirteen hours, much longer than my parents, or Dr. Engel, had anticipated. I'd lost a great amount of blood and needed a transfusion.

Dr. Engel had managed to close my ileostomy and create a new stoma. I'd have a second bag—my external bladder. But because of all the blood I'd lost, the plan to remove my bladder was scrapped. It was abandoned inside of me like an inflatable pool toy. Only this pool toy, I'd later find out, would collect bacteria, and because no signals went from my brain to tell my bladder it needed emptying, an infection would fester. In my late teens, this caused me to double over in pain. I'd need frequent bladder irrigations to relieve the pressure and stop infections.

A few days after my surgery, as he checked my incision, Dr. Engel told me I was making a fast recovery and that I'd be home by the 4th of July.

The day I was to leave, my mother stood in my hospital room, packing our clothes. I ran to the game room, only to find the girl with prosthetic legs standing in the middle of the hallway, arms folded against her chest. She wore a yellow dress, with yellow ribbons in her braided pigtails. When I told her I was going home she asked me to kiss her. I stood frozen in fear. "Give me a kiss goodbye," she demanded. I didn't know what else to do, so I made a retreat and ran back to my room and the safety of my mother, who, when I told her what had happened, chuckled.

Why was I so afraid to kiss this little girl who I'd spent hours drawing and playing with in the game room? Was it because she was Black? Did I fear that if my father found out, he would be mad? Or my grandma Irwin, who, when she found out I had a transfusion, asked, "What if they gave him a Negro's blood?" Decades later, I still think of the girl with the prosthetic legs, and I hope if she has any recollection of me or that day, she forgives me for being such a fool.

After two weeks in Johns Hopkins, I was going home. Even though the surgery hadn't gone as planned, I was no longer bound by diapers. Gerald and his wife Joann bought me a six-pack of briefs, my first pairs of underwear! Finally, I could also see and touch my penis! I felt like I was reborn, like anything was possible. It was a revelation.

The Monster in the Mirror

1981

When my mother and I arrived home from Johns Hopkins, we found our kitchen full of balloons. A banner hung across the cabinets with the words "Welcome Home" written in red bubble letters. In the bottom right corner was a cartoon of a bald man with a large nose and a gaping smile. This was "Buzz," a cartoon character drawn by our neighbor Ronnie, the same Ronnie who just a year earlier sat on our living room floor crying over his lost job and his alcoholism. He got all the kids in the neighborhood to sign their names on the banner.

A few days later, my nana's younger brother, Paul, and his wife, my aunt Angie, arrived from Cleveland, and with them a puppy: a white terrier I named Benji after the movie star. Benji was a compulsive humper who slept at the foot of my bed and sat with me when I watched television. When my mother took him in her arms, she'd serenade him, singing "The First Time Ever I Saw Your Face," and he'd gaze at her as if love-struck. Benji became my new best friend.

My surgery had gone well. I was cared for and loved. All was right in my world. Then, everything changed. My mother and I drove to Buffalo to meet with an ostomy nurse at a pharmacy. In an exam room, as she showed my mother several different ostomy products—skin barriers, wafers, pouches, tape—I stood naked in front of a full-length mirror, transfixed by my body, looking at it as if for the first time. A long scar, like a horizon line, started just above my right kidney and ran across my lower torso. It ended near my left pelvis. Like the scar to repair my esophagus, it had nearly cut me in half. My two stomas stuck out like two red blobs. As I stood there, piss ran from my urostomy down my right leg, and I watched myself cry.

Who was this creature reflecting back? This Quasimodo? This Elephant Man? Did my mother know I was a freak? A specimen to be poked and gawked at? Did my father? My grandparents? My friends at school? And why hadn't they told me? I'd always known I was different, but now it became clear: I was a monster. All the possibilities that seemed to be in reach a couple of weeks earlier vanished before my teary eyes. In that instant I knew the only way I could survive was to hide my body from the world.

That September I entered Ms. Locke's fifth grade class. In October, my parents, after being legally separated for two years, were officially divorced, nearly 13 years to the day after they became husband and wife.

My mother was forced to go back to work. She was hired part-time at U.S. News, a store that specialized in magazines, lottery tickets, and tobacco products. She worked afternoons and evenings, and though her job didn't provide health insurance or paid time off, the hours allowed her to volunteer at Saint Elizabeth's as a lunchroom monitor. Her boss let her take off whenever I had to go to the hospital, or if she needed to come to school and change my ostomy bags. It would be a few years before I learned to change them on my own.

Unfortunately, my urostomy bag leaked all the time, without warning, as if of its own will—with the same suddenness that my esophagus constricted. In only a matter of seconds a dark stain would spread across my pants, soaking me in my own piss. My mother, equipped with my ostomy supplies and a change of clothing, would take me into the girls' bathroom and lay me on a table across from the sink like she used to when she changed my diapers. It never used to bother me, but suddenly, I became self-conscious and paranoid. I could feel their eyes on me. Sometimes, I thought I heard them laughing, whispering about me and my piss-soaked pants.

This is not to say that my life was terrible, that I never had fun. Far from it. Most of the time, I was able to keep the monster in the mirror locked away somewhere deep in my psyche. My feelings of paranoia and self-loathing were few and far between, at least for a few more years, until puberty and all its discontents sent me reeling. My otherness made an easy target for mockery and abuse. Mostly, I enjoyed a greater sense of freedom—I rode my bike with Mike and JoJo, peddling with one foot (shedding my training wheels the summer before eighth grade). We'd go to U.S. News after school, and while my mother was busy with customers, we'd sneak over to the porno magazine aisle with our *Fangoria* and wrestling magazines as cover and gawk at the full-color photos of women who bared their breasts and vaginas. Mike and JoJo gasped and sighed and said words like pussy and clit, and I laughed as if I knew what it was all about.

I even took pride in my roles as mascot for the Seton Royals basketball team, and batboy for the Lakeside Club, where I scurried onto the field like an opossum to retrieve the discarded bats, my mother cheering me on from the bleachers.

A Slice of the American Dream

1981-1984

After my parents' divorce was made official and my mother returned to the workforce, we suddenly were labeled low income. Before this, I had no knowledge of my parents' financial situation. All I knew was that I was cared for and never lacked anything. Now that we were low income, we started receiving SSI (Supplemental Security Income), a federal program that gave monthly cash payments to the elderly and disabled to help them meet basic needs like food, clothing, and shelter. To keep receiving this money, however, we were made to go downtown to the Social Security Office periodically and suffer through an interview with Mr. Knowles, my appointed caseworker.

Before my mother and I even set foot in the Social Security Office she had to make sure our SSI renewal application was filled out correctly. The application required my mother to answer a series of questions relating to household demographics, as well as our economic situation. How many people lived in our house? Did we own or rent? If we owned, was there a mortgage, and if so who was responsible for it? They wanted to know if my mother was employed. If she answered yes, then they wanted to know if it was full-time or part-time. How many hours? How much did she earn? Did she pay utility bills? Did she own a car? It also asked questions about my disability. Was it permanent or short-term? Was it caused by an accident? My mother also had to include documents pertaining to all these questions. If she forgot to include any of them, or if she missed or incorrectly answered even one question, the whole process had to be started over.

Decades later, in my mother's papers, I found an envelope with one such form from the Chautauqua County Department of Health and Social Services, dated December 28, 1983. It said an appointment had been made for a financial evaluation to determine whether we would receive "payments of services" under the Physically Handicapped Children's Program. We were to report at 10:00 a.m. on Tuesday, January 24, 1984.

For this appointment, my mother was required to bring her income tax returns and eight weeks of paystubs (I don't know what she earned, but I imagine it wasn't much more than minimum wage, which was $3.35 an hour); bank account or savings statements (for which my mother wrote "none"); life insurance, stock, bond, or investment statements (all "none"); proof of health insurance; receipts for mortgage payments, house insurance, and house maintenance repairs (all paid by my father); as well as receipts for major medical expenses. On the back of this form, my mother wrote that at the end of February I would be admitted to Children's Hospital for treatment for possible peptic ulcers. Enclosed in the envelope was a final notice from National Fuel, dated April 23, 1983, for $680.61. There was also an agreement from a company called Bart's Services that required my mother to make a deposit before any repairs to our leaky roof would be made.

The Social Security Office was on Central Avenue, above West Drug, where we bought my ostomy supplies. A woman who wore wire-rim glasses and a stern expression worked at the pharmacy. When she spoke she sounded like a bird. She had a son named John, who my mother said was "retarded" like Rocky—the man who plopped action figures on his father's head during 7 p.m. Mass at Saint Elizabeth's. Though John was probably only ten years my senior, he looked like an old man. This might have been due to his quiff hairdo and the tight suits and bow ties he wore, or his big blue eyes that blinked like caution lights. His face always held a deep scowl, as if he'd just shit his pants. Sometimes, I'd see him in other stores, or in restaurants, his mother always hurrying him along, tugging on his elbow as if he were still a child. On the rare occasions when our eyes met, I felt a spark of recognition, as if we were bound together by a mutual fate. What I feared most, though I loved my mother fiercely, was that I'd end up like John or Rocky—that I'd spend the rest of my life following my mother around and would never be able to live on my own.

Inside the Social Security Office's lobby, my mother and I sat on wobbly plastic chairs and waited, along with other families who carried with them the same forms. The orange carpet that spread beneath us was stained and frayed at the edges. It was the same color as the powder the janitor at Saint Elizabeth's used to clean up puke in the cafeteria after someone ate too many tacos or pizza buns.

Once our number was called, we made our way through the maze of desks and filing cabinets until we reached Mr. Knowles' desk, tucked in a corner at the far end of a long room. It was illuminated by a single light bulb that hung from the ceiling, the kind you might find in some Eastern-Bloc interrogation room.

Mr. Knowles motioned for my mother and me to sit on the two metal chairs across from his desk. I soon became transfixed by the sight of his enlarged forehead and droopy hound-dog eyes that looked out from behind his thick-framed glasses. His fingernails, like my own, were bitten to the quick. Whenever he stretched his arms, I could see puddles of sweat that had soiled his armpits, the way piss darkened my pants whenever my ostomy bag leaked, and for a brief moment I felt sorry for him.

Time gnawed while Mr. Knowles groaned and stretched as he shuffled through our application. I picked my fingers until blood bloomed like a tiny flower at the corner of my left thumbnail. My mother stewed with impatience. I imagined she needed a cigarette or coffee. In my mind, I pictured her leaping from her chair like a panther and attacking him. To my disappointment she just looked at me and rolled her eyes.

My empathy for Mr. Knowles quickly vanished. Just the idea that he held our fate in his hands, that it was all up to him whether our application was approved or denied, or that he could take as long as he wanted and there was nothing we could do but wait, made me want to thrash him.

In the stale silence, as I watched the light reflect off his head, Mr. Knowles grunted. At that same instant, my mother's stomach gurgled. Then, suddenly, with a violent jolt, Mr. Knowles set the papers down and heaved a deep sigh.

"It appears that everything is in order," he exclaimed, staring at the empty space above our heads. "You're good for another year."

With that, my mother mumbled a thank you, grabbed her purse and threw me a *Let's-get-the-hell-out-of-here* look. Then we hurried down hallway, past the still crowded waiting room and into the fresh air, where my mother promptly lit a cigarette. In a week's time, we'd receive the confirmation letter along with our block of government cheese, our food stamps, and a monthly check for $640.

Naively, I thought that once my mother saved enough money, we would no longer have to sit like beggars in front of Mr. Knowles' desk, watching sweat turn his freshly starched shirts to mush, as he checked and rechecked every comma, decimal, and dollar sign on our application. For now, we were a little closer to the promised land, that shining city on a hill President Reagan spoke of with a twinkle in his eye. But my mother never managed to save any money, and we kept returning year after year, waiting, hoping, for our slice of the American Dream.

Born Again

1983-1984

The times they were a changin', and just as the surgery that freed me from diapers had transformed my life, my mother's newfound faith transformed hers. She became drenched to the bone in everything Jesus. She joined Kairos Prison Ministry and Cursillo, an apostolic movement of the Roman Catholic Church whose focus was teaching lay people how to be effective Christian leaders in their communities. This, along with her singing in Sam Mancuso's choir, our attending Mass in the evenings, and my serving as an altar boy, found us at church up to seven times per week, thus setting our lives on a beguiling trajectory.

My mother's Cursillo experience began with a three-night retreat. This meant we needed to find someone who was not only willing to take me in, feed me, and make sure I got to school, but also willing to change my ostomy bags.

Sam and Joanne Mancuso were those people. For me, it was a moment of profound surrender and trust. I'd have to reveal my body with all its deformities and scars. It was awkward and not without its moments of stress, and at times comical. At the age of ten, I'd not spent more than a night away form my mother. To say that it was awkward, that it was stressful, would be an undertatement, but it also had moments of comedy. The first night at the Mancuso's house, I lay in the darkness and quietly cried myself to sleep. But by the second evening, I was having fun playing with their youngest daughter, Ellyn. I will always love the Mancusos for the generosity and boundless kindness they showed me, and for giving my mother the opportunity to do something for herself, without having to worry about me.

Four days later, when my mother's retreat ended, she picked me up from school.

"I never felt love like that before," my mother said. "It was as if I was on fire, but at the same time at peace with everything." Though I couldn't understand what she meant, I could tell by the look in her eyes and the tone of her voice that something had changed. It was as if she'd broken free of some weight she'd been carrying.

As with everything she did, my mother embraced this new version of faith with genuine passion. Suddenly, we were thrust into a world populated by an odd assortment of characters—would-be spiritualists and born-agains, people who spoke in tongues, people who writhed as if possessed and claimed to have visited Hell, as well as people who broke into spontaneous song. My mother called it rapture, or ecstasy: a heightened spiritual awareness, like what her favorite saints Francis and Teresa of Avila, experienced.

As part of Kairos Prison Ministry my mother traveled to Collins Correctional Facility with the Mancusos and Jim and Sheila Sobkowski once a month to talk with and listen to inmates, hoping to impart on them some of that love and sense of peace she felt. One such person was a tall blonde-haired man who called himself Tex and claimed to have been part of the Manson family.

Around this time, my esophagus started constricting more and more. I missed big chunks of school and was forced to eat baby food, the only thing I could keep down. I was in and out of Children's Hospital, where Dr. Jewett dilated my esophagus more times than I could remember. This coincided with my

Rambo phase. I became obsessed with the idea of going off to war and dying. Jake Sobkowski, Jim and Sheila's son, became my new best friend. He also dreamed of joining the Army and going off to war.

A year older than me, Jake suffered from a debilitating disease that caused his hips to deteriorate. When he was in fourth grade, he had to have both his hips replaced. He was in a half-body cast for almost an entire year. Mrs. Wilkins, my third-grade teacher, whom I fell in love with after she taught me how to tie my shoelaces, used to carry Jake up and down Saint Elizabeth's four flights of stairs each day.

When Jake wasn't confined to a cast and I wasn't in the hospital, we ran through our neighborhoods at night dressed like ninjas, spying in windows and tying tripwire in strangers' backyards. We also put letters in my next-door neighbor Melvin Tilly's mailbox—after he called me a crippled bastard—letting him know he was under surveillance by the Junior Green Berets.

We visited Sergeant Turmain at the local army recruiting office and took home brochures. He answered our endless questions and shook his head in amusement as we narrated our naive fantasies. All this was a vast contradiction from my John Lennon and "Give Peace a Chance" ethos as well as anything Cursillo or Kairos stood for. Of course, my mother indulged me, as she always had. She let me believe I could do anything I set my mind to, even joining the Army. I couldn't even handle gym class; how did I ever expect to survive in the Army? Jake, on the other hand, despite his double hip replacement, would not only go on to join the Army, but serve three tours in Iraq over the course of both Gulf Wars.

Sometimes, we traveled with our mothers to Collins Correctional Facility, where his father and Sam Mancuso led a spiritual retreat for inmates. Before we arrived at the prison, however, we gathered in a church a few miles away, along with fifty or sixty others to pray and listen to former inmates testify about how they'd been saved. On one of these nights, a man named Paul took to the podium on the altar and spoke.

Paul was a member of the Seneca nation. He was a tall, pockmarked man who wore his long blue-black hair tied in a ponytail. In a soft-spoken voice, he told the congregation about the grocery store clerk he'd shot and killed during a robbery twenty years earlier.

"I used to be pretty angry and confused," he said. If it wasn't for Kairos, or Jesus' love and forgiveness, he didn't know what would have become of his life. I sat in stunned silence. I'd never been in the same room as a murderer before. As Paul continued, his voice cracked. He wiped his brow with the back of his hand and loosened his tie. "I was desperate," he admitted. "Desperate for something I couldn't put words to." I sat up straight to hear him better. "Many years would go by," he continued. "Many dark nights of the soul before I would be able to admit that what I was desperate for was love."

After his testimony, my mother and I drove to the prison. There, we found Jake and his mom, amid the crowd, next to a giant razor-wire fence. We stood side-by-side as rain poured down and our shoes sank in the wet grass. Every few minutes, a spotlight from a nearby guard tower swept across the perimeter. We were given candles, and after they were lit, someone started to sing "On Eagle's Wing"—a song whose words I knew from hearing my mother sing along to the record at home. Soon a line of prisoners came into view on the opposite side of the fence, with Jake's father and Sam, who strummed an acoustic guitar, in the lead. After the songs a prayer followed, then a loud, collective amen rang out from both sides of the fence and everyone clapped and shouted. We watched the line of prisoners disappear into the night, returning from where they'd come from, then walked back to our cars and went home.

Jake and I were always forced to attend Kairos' monthly potluck dinners, which were held at different members' houses. Decked out in our thrift-store army fatigues and green berets, we hunkered down in a far corner of the room with our plates of pasta salad, Jell-O, and potato chips, and thumbed through the pages of coffee-table-sized books that chronicled World War II and Vietnam—pictures of bombs and blood and death. We pretended we couldn't hear the adults, with their out-of-tune voices, and their raucous proclamations of faith.

"Tell me, do you love Jesus?" a choir of women asked (my mother and Jake's mother among them).

"Yes, I love Jesus," Jake's father responded.

"Do you really love Jesus?"

"Yes, I really love Jesus!"

"Can you tell me how much you love Jesus?"

"This much," Jake's father proclaimed, and stretched out his arms crucifixion style.

I admit I was embarrassed by these public displays of faith—sing-alongs, holding hands, praying. It all seemed corny, and a bit false, especially when my mother tried to get me to join in. Yet, there was something about those nights that made me feel good, and I admired the way my mother was trying to reinvent herself.

My Mother Disguised as Little Bo Peep Has an Announcement

Friday, January 4, 2019

My cell phone chimed at one in the afternoon while I was at work checking a patient in at the urology clinic. Seeing my aunt Stephanie's name on my cell screen, I immediately thought the worst: my mother had another stroke, or she'd died. It had only been two days since I left my mother in her apartment, in the care of hospice nurses and aides.

"Your mom fainted today while me and Uncle Joe were visiting," my aunt said. Her voice sounded stressed. "Actually, she fainted three or four times."

My aunt said she and my uncle had been at my mother's apartment for the past two hours. My mother seemed okay now. The hospice nurse and social worker had already come and gone, and promised to return the following morning.

"Come as soon as you can," my aunt urged.

*

When Jenny and I arrived four hours later, we found my aunt and uncle sitting on the couch, and my mother on the love seat with a blanket thrown over her legs. Something about her seemed different, but I couldn't tell what.

"Hi Jay," she said, her voice quiet and hoarse.

"How are you feeling, Mom?"

"I'm fine, just resting."

"You got a haircut," I said, realizing what looked different about her. Though her hair still had its sangria coloring, her punky, Pat Benatar spikes were gone. In their place were curled bangs that made her look like Little Bo Peep.

Then my aunt blurted out, "Your mother's worried you'll quit your job," as if it were a secret she'd been waiting all day to tell me.

Where did that come from? My uncle put up his hands as if to say, "Don't look at me."

*

In my teenage years and early twenties, I'd acquired a reputation as a slacker. I admit I had it in my head that because of my disabilities, I should be immune from having to work, even though everyone around me—my grandfather, aunt, uncle, my father, my mother, all worked. Still, I couldn't remember quitting a job just because I didn't want to work. From my senior year in high school through my thirties, I worked at grocery stores, in offices, bookstores, and even as a substitute teacher. I did quit one of the grocery jobs when I was twenty-eight, though, to have more time to write, this with my mother's full support and encouragement. I also quit a job to go to Ireland when was twenty-five.

My grandfather, who came of age during the Great Depression, could not understand my "gallivanting," as he called it, my wanting to see the world. He never tired of yelling at me, of telling me to settle down and become a teacher. In his mind, teachers had it made. He'd go on about how easy it was—evenings and summers free, not to mention holidays.

My uncle Joe would egg him on, just to hear him rant and rave, knowing my grandfather dished out the same spiel to him when he was a young, aspiring artist. "He doesn't want to work," my uncle would say, and wink in my direction.

"I know it," my grandfather would roar. "He just wants to grow his hair long, get drunk, and read those books of his. You can't tell him nothin'. Goes in one ear and out the other."

"I told him he should be a teacher," my uncle replied. "But he doesn't wanna hear it. He says, teaching is for losers!" And with that, my grandfather would explode in a choking fit of rage, spit and tobacco flying from his pipe, while my uncle, satisfied with himself, sat laughing.

*

Now, approaching late middle age, about to get married for the second time, I knew that whether I liked it or not, I needed a job with good health insurance. I had no plans of quitting, I assured everyone, at least until I found another job—or won some prestigious literary prize, and what were the chances of that happening? As much as I still dreamed of the bohemian life—living in squalor in some flophouse in Greenwich Village, Dublin, or Paris—I no longer found the starving-artist life romantic.

With that settled, my mother said she had an announcement to make. She'd come to the hard realization, she said, that she was no longer able to stay in her apartment alone. Even with Sherri coming every day, it wasn't enough. She needed around-the-clock care, and with my having to work, she decided it was best she move to Pittsburgh.

*

The first time I tried to find my mother a place to live in

Pittsburgh, it was in 2011. She called to tell me that she could no longer afford to live in her house. "Whatever," she scoffed, "I'll just live in the woods."

"Whatever!" she'd say, whenever we talked about her health, her finances, her house, or about moving. It was as if she'd resigned herself to whatever fate had in store.

The breaking point came one day when, according to my mother, water shot out of the toilet in the basement like a cannon and the washing machine started leaking. "It was a sign," she proclaimed. Though whether it was from God or the devil, she didn't know.

Once my mother agreed to leave her house, all it took was a single phone call. I reached out to Dan Reininga. His family owned many apartments in Dunkirk, including the Lincoln Arms, a four-story apartment building for seniors and those with low-income. It was on Main Street, a few blocks from where I'd grown up. My mother had first met Dan's father, Pete, in the 60s when she worked for Brooks Hospital and went door-to-door to local businesses asking for donations for the hospital's various campaign drives.

Dan told me there was an immediate opening. Since it was a participating HUD building, my mother's rent would be subsidized according to her income. He also agreed to waive the usual credit check, which my mother and I both knew she wouldn't pass.

My mother moved in the weekend after Mother's Day in 2013. I didn't help her, which became a source of contention for years. I had just visited on Mother's Day. My first wife, Leilani, and I had separated, and I was living in an efficiency apartment, working at the Job Corps for $11.45 an hour. Leilani kept our car since I couldn't afford the payments. Anytime I wanted to visit my mother, I had to rent a car, which cost up to $400 for a weekend. Whether this registered with my mother or not, I don't know. I had the feeling she assumed I'd just move back home and live with her again after Leilani and I split up.

"We're exhausted," my mother said, referring to her and her friend Jeanette, when I called to see how the move went. "We moved carload after carload."

I still regret that I didn't go up to help my mother move, even if it meant renting a car two weekends in a row. She was in reasonably good health then, but I let her move knowing she couldn't afford to hire movers and had to rely on the help of friends.

*

Not long after my mother put her house up for sale, the real estate agent backed out of the deal when he discovered there was a lien on the property due to my mother's credit card debt and unpaid back taxes. Three years later the house was sold at auction for a fraction of what we originally paid. After her stroke in 2016, my mother agreed to move to Pittsburgh but insisted on living in her own apartment. She even promised to quit smoking. The government implemented a no-smoking policy in all HUD housing. She had continued to smoke at the Lincoln Arms and even received a few complaints but was fortunate that the landlord and most of the other residents turned a blind eye. If she moved into a new building, however, she'd absolutely have to give up her cigarettes.

Good news arrived in November 2017: there was an opening at an apartment complex on Pittsburgh's South Side. The third-floor apartment had high ceilings, a handicapped-accessible bathroom, lots of light from the windows, and a balcony in the communal room. The woman who gave me a tour called after a few days and said my mother's application had been accepted. "Please let me know ASAP," she said. "We can hold the room for a week, two at most."

The building was a ten-minute drive from our apartment. Until she was approved under HUD for reduced rent, Jenny and I agreed to cover the cost over what she usually paid. It seemed easy. It seemed like everything was going to work out (though we feared she'd continue smoking and be evicted).

When I called my mother, I told her I'd drive up and help her pack. I'd help her find new doctors. I told her it would all work out, that we'd get to see each other more often. However, when I told my mother that they wouldn't hold the apartment for long, that she'd have to make a decision soon, she became angry.

"This is my life we're talking about," she snapped. "You act as if it's easy, like there's nothing to it."

"I'm not like you," she said. "I can't just pick up and leave whenever I want. And without even seeing the place? Really? I don't think so."

In the end my mother chose to stay in Dunkirk.

*

Now my mother had decided to move in with Jenny and me. I was glad that I'd be able to take care of her, but there was the issue of my mother's smoking. The thought of breathing in that smoke every day, of having it on my clothes, made me sick. I was sure my mother would be living with us for several months, maybe longer. Besides her smoking, I was also worried that once things were set in place, she'd change her mind and want to stay in Dunkirk.

But this time was different. This time my mother had cancer, and whether or not I chose to admit it, she was not going to get better. Moving to Pittsburgh was not just her best option, it was her only one.

A Flicker of Flame

Sunday, January 6, 2019

Two days after my mother announced her decision to move to Pittsburgh, Jenny went home to get our apartment ready for my mother's arrival. The plan was for her to return on Wednesday after she fixed up our back room, which had been Jenny's office, with all the things my mother claimed she couldn't live without. These vital possessions included a bookcase, end table, paintings and photographs, as well as the multi-colored rug (à la Matisse, or late-period Picasso) my mother originally bought for the "Elvis Room," an addition to our house on Fifth Street, which she paid for with the money she received after my grandfather died. The room was filled with her Elvis and Kennedy memorabilia.

Until then, I'd stay with my mother and coordinate with the Dunkirk and Pittsburgh hospice offices to ensure a smooth transition. I'd been approved for FMLA, which meant I could take off any time I needed without losing my job, but those days would be unpaid. With Jenny working from home and hospice coming in, we both agreed that I'd save my days off for when things got really bad, which we naively believed wouldn't be anytime soon. I still held out hope that once my mother settled in and became comfortable, once we developed a routine, she might feel better. Maybe she'd even feel strong enough to go for a ride, or out to dinner.

The first night, after Jenny left, my mother and I listened to the oldies station with the lights dimmed like votive candles. I thought of my nana, and how glamorous she always seemed, until cancer struck.

I remembered watching my mother, aunt Stephanie, and Geraldine hold my nana's body as it writhed with seizures, and how her lips bubbled with foam and her eyes rolled back in her head.

When this happened, my grandfather locked himself in the bathroom and turned on the faucets. Above the din I could hear his muffled sobs.

When the seizures stopped, the house felt quiet as church.

After a while, my grandfather would emerge from the bathroom and return to his armchair in front of the television, where he proceeded to rant and rave at the Yankee game. "Jesus' Whiskers Alive," he howled, as if he were alone in the room, condemning "those bums" who couldn't even "hit the ball out of the infield."

My Nana Was the Glamorous Type

1981-1989

"I'm Robin Hood," I yelled, and thrust my plastic sword at my nana. "I've come to steal from the rich and give to the poor!" Then I raided the candy drawer, which was crammed full of Kit-Kat bars, Three Musketeers, Reese's Peanut Butter Cups, and marshmallow circus peanuts. No matter how much I took, the drawer's contents never diminished. The fridge and freezer were the same: 16-ounce glass bottles of RC Cola and 7UP, my grandfather's "Dago meats," sliced provolone cheese, ice cream sandwiches, and popsicles, all for the taking.

What I enjoyed most those summer days, or days after school while my mother worked, was being the center of my nana's universe, and her willingness to give in to all my demands. In between her endless routine of cooking and cleaning and putting on makeup, we played games like tic-tac-toe, fifty-two card pickup, and Atari Pong. Looking back, I realize how fortunate my mother and I were. We may not have had a village to help us, but if it weren't for my grandparents, I don't know what we'd have done.

My nana also hung all my drawings on her kitchen wall. I'd been drawing for as long as I could remember. Before my father moved out, my parents paid for me to take formal art lessons with Barny Kasara, who lived across the street from us. Each Saturday morning, I'd spend two hours learning the rudiments of drawing and water-color painting. Among the small class of budding artists, I was by far the youngest. Yet, my tenure lasted just a few months. To say I was impatient, or that I preferred to run before I could walk, was an understatement and would characterize my future creative endeavors for the rest of my life. Or, as my mother liked to remind me, I had a fierce dislike for being told what and how to do anything. In my mind, learning the rudiments only served to slow me down. The fact that my nana so proudly displayed my artwork—cowboys being massacred by Indians, King Kong atop the Empire State Building, Rocky Balboa bruised and bloodied, raising his fists in victory, or Jesus, also gruesomely bloody, hanging from his cross—only proved my genius.

What I wanted was to be like my uncle Joe. He was a brilliant artist who lived the bohemian life in Boston and New York City before marrying my aunt Stephanie and working his way up to become the head of Human Resources at a local juice factory.

Another of my obsessions that my nana indulged was the news. By the age of ten or eleven, I was a seasoned news junkie. I watched Buffalo's Eyewitness News with Irv Weinstein, Don Postles, Rick Azar, and weatherman Tom Jolls with an almost religious fervor. I closely followed the plight of journalist and Western New York native Terry Anderson, who was being held hostage by Hezbollah in Lebanon, as well as that of Polish Solidarity leader Lech Wałęsa, who dared defy the evil Soviet Union, fighting for rights and better wages for himself and other workers in the Gdańsk shipyard. I also followed the .22 Caliber Killer, who, in the early 1980s, terrorized the citizens of Buffalo with a series of murders. There was also the oil glut, caused by a surplus in crude oil after the 1970s energy crisis, which my father blamed on Jimmy Carter.

One evening, the news reported that people in Western New York drove across the Peace Bridge into Canada to buy cheaper gas. That's when I decided to write a letter to President Reagan, who had recently survived an assassination attempt.

It was my nana who put pen to paper and wrote down the

words I dictated. She was the one who addressed the envelope to the White House, affixed a stamp, and instructed my grandfather to drop it in a mailbox.

A month later I received an envelope from the White House, postmarked April 29th, 1981. The letter was from President Reagan's Director of Correspondence, Ann Higgins. On a sheet of paper with White House letterhead, she thanked me for my concern about a "national problem that affects people of all ages: inflation," and encouraged me and all young people to "try to earn their money rather than expect their parents to give it to them." Did this mean I had to return the $5 allowance my nana stuffed into my hands each week? Even at ten years old, capitalism and socialism wrestled like cartoon angels and devils on my shoulders. In future years, I'd write to various presidents and government officials voicing my discontent about the old ship of state.

Sometimes I wondered if all the indulgences my nana showered on me, treating me as if I were a fragile jewel, were because of my many deformities and the fact that I was in and out of the hospital all the time. Yet, she also had a way of putting me in my place, of stomping on my dreams before they had a chance to bloom. When I'd talk about being a rockstar, or artist, and living in New York City like my uncle Joe, she'd scoff and tell me it was only a pipe dream. Maybe she was just trying to prevent me from being disappointed. I imagine that she and everyone in my family believed I'd have to be looked after my entire life. What I didn't know at the time was that my nana, the youngest of ten children, had her own dreams of being an artist, and a movie star like Sophia Loren, who, like my nana's parents, had come from Naples. These dreams would go unfulfilled. At age sixteen, my nana dropped out of school to work in a factory. Then, she married my grandfather four years later.

What I was certain of, besides her undying devotion, was that she was glamorous. Everything about her was glamorous. She not only enjoyed being the center of attention, but she seemed to crave it. She showed this in how she dressed—Nehru pantsuits, high-heeled shoes, and costume jewelry, which she wore every day, even if that day was spent (as most of her days were) cooking and cleaning and chasing after me.

Every room in her house was immaculate, like a department store showroom or museum diorama—from the exacting way in which she arranged pillows on the couch to the doilies and cherub figurines on the end tables and the drapes that hung from windows she never opened lest the wind blow in any dust. Yet looking back, it all seemed like a facade to hide the fact that she was frightened of the world. Like Blanche DuBois in *A Streetcar Named Desire*, my nana hid behind a mystique of luxuriance.

My nana loved soap operas, *The Price is Right*, Johnny Carson, the Home Shopping Network, and *The Muppet Show*. She was an avid reader of such scandalous weeklies as *The National Enquirer* and *People Magazine*. She attended Mass each week and bowled, along with my grandfather, in a senior citizens' league. To all who knew her, my nana was the living embodiment of those 1950s matriarchs: Barbara Billingsley, Harriet Nelson, and Donna Reed. It was only after her death that I found out about a dark side, one that she kept hidden from my cousins and me, a dark side that my mother and uncle hid from us as well.

Yet, those afternoons and evenings I spent with my nana, warmed by her boundless love, made me believe I was special, that my life really did have a purpose.

"I'm Robin Hood," I yelled as I slid across the kitchen's red carpet and my nana feigned fear and awe, raising her arms in mock surrender.

Sickness Will Surely Take the Mind

Monday, January 7, 2019

My mother sat on her hospital bed staring out the window as I thumbed through the little red book where she'd chronicled all my deformities, hospitalizations, and surgeries, as well as all my firsts: first words, first steps, and first haircut.

As I was about to turn the page, one sentence stopped me: *Between 1971 and 1984,* it said in my mother's familiar blue script, *Jason had close to 280 esophagus dilations. During Lent in 1983, he became very ill and almost died.*

"Two hundred and eighty dilatations?" I exclaimed. "Is that true?"

"Don't you remember?" my mother asked. "You were out of school for most of seventh and eighth grade."

That spring, before I turned twelve, I'd lost a lot of weight and felt lethargic. At one point, unable to keep food down, my mother was forced to feed me shot glasses of 7UP every twenty minutes to keep me hydrated. Dr. Jewett had been dilating my esophagus every other week for months, which kept me in the hospital for three to four days after every dilatation. The effects of the anesthesia made me sick for even longer. Its foul odor—a mix of epoxy and Play-Doh—would follow me for decades like a demon conjured from the abyss of my psyche. Its long, slimy Hydra head would climb up my throat like bile every time I entered a hospital or doctor's office, causing me to gag or vomit.

Dr. Jewett suggested we see a colleague of his, a new, younger doctor who he hoped might be able to help. Dr. Cooney had a pudgy face and a mess of blond, stringy hair. The first time he was scheduled to dilate my esophagus, he didn't show up to the operating room and my surgery was postponed until the following week. My mother and I arrived at the hospital the night before. We were in the elevator, on our way to the snack bar, when the doors opened, and Dr. Cooney stumbled in. "What are you guys doing here?" he asked, his voice rising in surprise. We could smell booze on his breath. My mother flew into a rage and raised holy hell with hospital administration, the way she yelled at Sister Maurene, the principal at Saint Elizabeth's, who suggested I be sent to an institution rather than register for kindergarten. After that episode, we never saw Doctor Cooney again.

Being in the hospital wasn't always bad. I enjoyed all the attention and gifts I received. I made friends with some of the other patients as well as the nurses. My favorite nurse was Jill. Together we ran down the hallway, slow-motion style, she pretending to be Jaime Sommers, The Bionic Woman, and I, Steve Austin, The Six Million Dollar Man, both of us making the *chac-chac* sound of our bionic limbs.

After dilating my esophagus for what must have been the tenth time since January, Dr. Jewett took my mother aside and admitted that the dilations weren't working. He said he didn't know what else to do. He told her to pray for a miracle.

This my mother kept hidden, and I didn't understand how dire my situation really was until JoJo showed up at our kitchen door, all sweaty and out of breath, like those nights when we were in second grade and he'd bang on the door, wanting to use the phone to call around to local bars in search of his parents.

"Mr. Miller told the class that you're going to die soon!" he yelled.

*

Dr. Jewett gave the dilations another try, and even though I was sick for a week afterward from the anesthesia and a swollen throat, it seemed to work. I was able to eat solid foods again—pizza and cheeseburgers and potato chips, canned asparagus, and hot dogs. Little by little, I regained my strength. Was it a miracle? Due to my mother's faith? The army of saints she prayed to? Or the dedicated work of doctors and nurses?

Miracle or not, the effects were short-lived. My esophagus was okay for a while, and I was able to go back to school in the fall and start 7th grade, but it wasn't long before I found myself unable to swallow food again. I spent most of that year and a good chunk of 8th grade in and out of the hospital. That's when Mrs. Colletti came into my life.

She was married to Mr. Colletti, an undertaker who, years later, would be accused of burying poor people in cardboard boxes. He was also rumored to prowl the hallways of Brooks Hospital, trying to drum up business from family members of dying patients. I hoped she had no knowledge of these things. She certainly didn't mention them to me or my mother those afternoons she tutored me.

Mrs. Colletti and I would sit at the dining room table for a couple of hours those afternoons and go over division and fractions, the Constitution, and The Beatitudes. She'd make me diagram sentences and recite the names of the planets.

I marveled at how the overhead light reflected in her green eyes, and the little laugh lines that bloomed at the corners of her mouth when she smiled. Sometimes, when she wore a short-sleeved blouse, I maneuvered my chair to try to catch a glimpse of her breasts or a whiff of the perfume she wore. Sitting next to her, I felt a warmth spread throughout my body and a tightness grip my groin. Even though she was almost old enough to be my mother and married to Mr. Colletti, I fantasized that one day she'd see past my age, my constricting esophagus, my ostomies and clubfoot, and fall hopelessly in love, and we'd run away together to someplace exotic like Tahiti or Newark.

When I felt well enough, I returned to school for a few days a week and even attended my 8th-grade class party, which was held at the police department clubhouse (a few of my classmates' fathers were cops). When I arrived, there were no adults present, just my classmates, and they were all holding big plastic cups of foamy beer, laughing, and making out with one another. They all looked familiar, but somehow, they were all different. They gawked at me as if I were a time traveler—some vague version of myself from a past they'd long ago outgrown.

That Christmas, my mother bought me two gifts: a 45 record of "Do They Know It's Christmas?" by Band-Aid—an all-star recording to raise money for victims of the famine in Ethiopia—and a Yamaha classical guitar. After putting $50 down at Crino's Music Store, she paid $10 a week until the guitar was paid off. She also signed me up for lessons with Tom Gestwicki, who was the leader of his own folk choir at Saint Elizabeth's, which performed at 12 p.m. on Sundays.

The first song I learned was "Aura Lee," a Civil-War-era song whose melody Elvis borrowed for "Love Me Tender"—my mother's favorite song.

A few months after I began taking lessons, Tom invited me to join his choir. It was in his choir that I met Jodi, who sang and played the flute. I became smitten with her freckles and long red hair. Jodi was a year older than me and went to public school.

After we exchanged phone numbers, we talked every

evening, sometimes for hours. She told me about her dreams of becoming an Olympic gymnast, and I told her I wanted to be a rock star.

Then, one Sunday, a couple weeks later, barely into the second song, I realized that I couldn't keep up with the other guitarists, Jodi's older brother John among them. I couldn't play in time, and I found it impossible to finger some of the chords, like F major and B7. It was humiliating. As with my art lessons, I quit the folk choir after a few weeks, and Jodi and I lost touch forever.

Even though I was no longer a part of the choir, I continued with my guitar lessons. The following summer I watched Jimmy Page on TV as he swaggered across the stage at Live Aid. It was a revelation. I did my best to learn "Stairway to Heaven" and "Whole Lotta Love," and practiced his stagger and pout in the bathroom mirror for weeks, the way I imagined my father practiced Clint Eastwood's side-eye. Rock 'n' roll had become, for me, what Cursillo and Kairos were for my mother. She had her saints, and now, I had my own: John Lennon, Bob Dylan, Jimmy Page, and Pete Townshend. Their songs and albums became my new gospel. Rock 'n' roll had the power to change the whole world, and if not the whole world, then at least my world.

If Jimmy Page taught me to look like a guitar god, and John Lennon was a voice crying in the wilderness who turned me on to new ways of seeing and thinking, then it was Pete Townshend and his rock opera *Tommy*, about a deaf, dumb, and blind boy/pinball prodigy, who became a messiah for disaffected youth, who made me believe that the world beyond my bedroom window, beyond my hometown, was attainable for someone like me.

I couldn't say how, but *Tommy* made me feel less alone. I

could lose myself listening to Townshend's power chords and poetry, the way I lost myself studying maps in my world atlas, imagining all the places I'd travel to one day.

Sickness will surely take the mind, he sang, *where minds can't usually go*, and I knew he was singing to me. I was ready to take that amazing journey, to see all there was to see, and learn all there was to know. All I had to do was believe in myself and smash the mirror.

The Ouija Board Predicts My Death

1984

Christmas. We were all gathered at my house on Main Street—my mother, me, my grandparents, my aunt Stephanie and uncle Joe, and my cousins Aiesha and her younger sister, Amanda.

Aiesha was named after Muhammad's favorite wife, when my uncle was deep in his Muslim phase. A year younger than me, she was my best friend and my partner in crime, as well as the keeper of my secrets. The most important secret was that she promised never to tell my mother about all the times I puked because my esophagus constricted, knowing my fear of having to go to the hospital.

After dinner, Aiesha and I rushed to the den to listen to the 45 record "Do They Know It's Christmas?" that my mother had given me. After four or five listens, we grew tired, and Aiesha took out her Christmas present: a Ouija board. While my grandfather and uncle Joe snoozed in front of the television, and my mother, aunt Stephanie, and nana gossiped over coffee and cigarettes in the dining room, Aiesha and I asked the Ouija to divine our futures.

"Dear Ouija," Aiesha asked, her eyes scrunched up in concentration. "Are there more presents for me?" *No* was Ouija's response. "Will I get married? Will I be happy?" she asked.

Yes, Yes, the Ouija replied.

When it was my turn, I asked the Ouija board how old I would be when I died. Our hands hovered over the heart-shaped plastic game piece as it glided across the board, stopping on the numbers 4 and 1. I asked the date of my death, and the

Ouija answered, *September 29*. If I were to die at age forty-one, that meant it would be on September 29, 2012. When, finally, I asked how I would die, the game piece guided our hands over the letters M, B, and D.

Confused, I ran to my mother and asked if she knew what M.B.D. stood for, without telling her anything else. "Multiple birth defects!" she blurted out, as if answering the prize-winning question on some TV gameshow.

I was in shock, but acted as if nothing were wrong. How could I confess what I'd asked the Ouija board? Or what it replied? It would remain a secret between Aiesha and me.

Yet, the Ouija's prophecy only confirmed what I'd long suspected: that I was doomed, and that God was trying to kill me. Aiesha would get married and live happily ever after, while I would die at 41, not from an assassin's bullet, not in war, but from my own birth defects.

It was as if I had a timebomb inside me: twenty-six years, nine months, and counting.

Some nights, as I lay in bed, I swear I could hear it ticking, like a metronome, or the rain that dripped from our leaky roof. Or maybe it was just the beating of my wrong-sided, backward heart, hovering somewhere between my pectoral girdle and sternum.

Spaghetti Sundays

1980 - 1989

Sundays, we all gathered at my grandparents' house for spaghetti, which was served at 1 p.m. sharp. By the time my mother and I arrived, my nana, dressed to the nines in her high heels and costume jewelry, had already been hard at work for several hours preparing her "homemade" sauce—an eccentric concoction of Contadina tomato paste, pureed tomatoes, one or two jars of Ragu, and plenty of water. Added to this were Italian sausage, hunks of meatballs, thick slices of pepperoni, and three or four hard-boiled eggs. For dessert, she served a Banquet frozen pie: lemon meringue, chocolate graham cracker, or butterscotch.

While my nana moved from room to room in frantic jolts like a wind-up toy, making sure everything was just right, my mother and aunt Stephanie set the table, as my grandfather, already seated at the head of the table, devoured a heaping plate of spaghetti, which he washed down with a splash of "Dago Red." When he finished, he moved to the living room and planted himself in his favorite armchair in front of the television—a mammoth, oak-trimmed Zenith—to watch the Yankees, the Buffalo Bills, bowling, or whatever sporting event happened to be on. At his side, a pocket-sized transistor radio was tuned to a separate sporting event. When the rest of us finally sat down to eat—my mother, me, Aunt Stephanie, Uncle Joe, Aiesha, and Amanda—my grandfather, ever the armchair coach, could be heard in the next room, yelling over the din of the TV. Yet his yelling was brief, for he'd soon fall asleep and begin snoring.

After dinner, my uncle Joe, pretending to be Dracula, his

hands hanging in the air like bat wings, chased Aiesha and me around the house. "I vant to bite your neck! I vant to taste your blood," he hissed in mock Bela Lugosi style, and we'd fall down in hysterics, then lock ourselves in the bathroom, only to reemerge ten minutes later begging him to do it again. This, of course, set my nana's nerves on edge, fearful we'd injure ourselves, or just wanting quiet. She did her best to corral us, bribing us with candy or slices of pie, which we gobbled like urchins.

After eating our dessert, Aiesha and I, with Amanda in tow, would make our escape, running upstairs. In my mother's girlhood bedroom, whose walls were painted Pepto Bismol pink (my uncle's adjoining room painted a chalky blue), we opened the armoire and exhumed the old photo albums, studying them like artifacts—fragments from a time long gone. There were hundreds of photos scattered on the armoire's floor; photos chronicling our grandparents' early years: my grandfather in swimming trunks carrying my grandmother on the beach, photos of their wedding, photos of them in Las Vegas with my uncle Paul and aunt Angie, who gave me my dog Benji when I returned home from Johns Hopkins Hospital; photos in Quebec and New York City. There were photos of my mother and uncle as children, my mother with her hair in braids, squinting at the camera, my uncle wearing my grandfather's long coat and fedora.

Our favorite photos were those Polaroids that featured Aiesha and me (my grandfather had lost his flair for taking photographs by the time Amanda was born). There was one of me carrying my grandfather's lunch pail, one of Aiesha in her *Welcome Back, Kotter* T-shirt, ribbons of toilet paper tied in her hair. Another of the two of us posing in our new Easter outfits: me holding my doll Timmy and Aiesha with a stuffed monkey.

When we grew exhausted from the photo albums, we'd rush downstairs and pull the slimy cord of the flower-shaped, plastic music box that hung on the kitchen door. The melody that escaped sounded like a cross between a nursery rhyme and a horror movie soundtrack. We pulled the string over and over until one of our parents begged us to stop.

No matter what we did, every time Aiesha and I got together, it was an adventure. Some Sundays, we sat on the floor scribbling in our notebooks, drawing and writing poems. When it was warm out, we explored the neighborhood, sometimes walking to Holy Trinity Cemetery—where our nana's side of the family was buried—to frolic among the tombstones.

Yet, other times, we stayed put and sat with adults at the dining room table, under a cloud of cigarette smoke while our mothers and nana gossiped or played board games. If my uncle was in the right mood, he'd tell a story from his youth or his college years at Youngstown State, where he studied art. I sat in awe listening to his talk of gangsters and prize fighters, Dean Martin and Sinatra. The stories I loved most, however, were the ones from his time living in Boston and New York City—what my mother referred to as his "Lost Years" from 1966-70.

"We didn't know where he was," my mother claimed. "He just disappeared." Then, Father Bernardo from Holy Trinity received a letter from a priest in Boston telling him that he'd just married my uncle and his young bride, Jorita. Jorita was Black, and this caused a rift between my uncle and grandfather.

"Grandpa cried all the time," my mother said. "It was Nana who begged him to take your uncle back."

After my uncle and Jorita divorced, he moved to New York City, where he worked at a garment factory and attended meetings of the Young Socialists in Union Square, falling under the charismatic spell of Chairman Mao and Che Guevara.

I never tired of hearing his stories: about the time he met Muhammad Ali, the time he tried to join the Black Muslims, how he handed out pamphlets for the Black Panthers, how he was followed by the FBI, who had accused him of being a communist. Then, there was the story of how he and my aunt Stephanie met and their early courtship, not long after he returned home from New York City in the fall of 1970.

"It was at BJ's bar," he'd say. "I used to call her Big Red. Then, one day, when I was living at the Hotel Lafayette in Buffalo, she just showed up with all her belongings. What could I do?" My uncle bellowed in exaggerated amusement as my aunt slapped his hand and blushed.

From my young, impressionable perspective, my uncle Joe was everything I dreamed of being—a brilliant artist whose canvases included cityscapes, portraits of my aunt, as well as portraits of the music, sports stars, and mobsters he idolized. Some of his paintings were exhibited at the Boxing and Baseball Halls of Fame. To me, he was a revolutionary, a dyed-in-the-wool bohemian, the coolest, most fascinating person I had ever met. It was my uncle Joe who first turned me on to the likes of Vincent van Gogh, John Lee Hooker, and Malcolm X. I also admired his generosity and humor. Always joking, it is his humor, most of all, that resonates.

It was my nana, however, who drew us all together. She was the beacon that provided light. Yes, she worried. Yes, she was neurotic, but wasn't that how grandmothers were supposed to be? She once told Aiesha and me that if we went to the park, the old women who lived in the woods would kidnap and eat us. She made my grandfather drive her to and from her weekly hairdresser appointments, even though it was only a block from their house. She wouldn't be caught dead in a store by herself, or seen sitting on her own front porch, lest the neighbors think she was mad. But she showered us with love and affection. What more could we ask for?

That's why I was shocked when, during the summer I turned sixteen, my mother accused my nana of faking when she claimed she'd been experiencing chest pains and having trouble breathing. "She's just doing it for the attention," my mother scoffed. "She's jealous."

At the time, my grandfather had been diagnosed with breast cancer, and was recovering from a mastectomy at Roswell Park Hospital in Buffalo. I would later learn that when my mother was in high school, bedridden for almost a year with anemia and scoliosis, my nana mysteriously developed the same symptoms.

This time, however, she was not faking. Doctors found a tumor on one of her kidneys. They removed it, but the cancer had already metastasized to her lungs and brain.

One day, a few months before my nana died, I visited her, bringing a cassette player and a tape of "Stairway to Heaven" by Led Zeppelin. She'd always liked the song, but on this day, lying in the hospital bed my grandfather had grudgingly bought and had set up in the living room, she became angry. How could I have been so naive? My nana may have liked the song before, but now, after losing her hair, no longer able to stand, or control her own body, playing a song about a stairway to heaven no doubt only reminded her of the little time she had left. In that awkward moment, as I stood beside her bed, our eyes locked. "Look at me," she almost shouted. "I'm as useless as you."

Was this the cancer talking, or did she really believe I was useless? Had she always believed this? I kept that afternoon a secret for decades, never admitting to anyone what she'd said, just like I'd kept the knowledge of my monstrosity a secret after viewing my naked body in the pharmacist's mirror.

After my nana died, my mother and uncle Joe began telling stories about their childhoods. They poured out like a monsoon. These were not the stories Aiesha and I had grown up hearing—about holidays and road trips to New York City and Youngstown. Instead, they were horror stories about the neglect and abuse she and my uncle endured from my nana.

"It went on for years," my mother claimed. "But back then everything was always hush-hush." She said that whatever went on inside the house, stayed there, a dirty secret.

"We didn't say anything to anyone," she said. "Besides, who would believe us?"

Family Secrets

Tuesday, January 8, 2019

"I hope you don't think less of me," my mother said, as she lit a cigarette. Outside the sliding glass door, the sky looked like concrete. Smokey Robinson sang "My Girl" on the oldies station.

"I tried to kill myself," she continued. "I took a handful of sleeping pills when I was eighteen." Regretting her decision, my mother called her aunt Rose, who rushed over with her husband Neff and took my mother to the emergency room. My grandparents were in Las Vegas.

"I just couldn't take living with Nana anymore. I don't know how I would have survived without Aunt Rose," she sighed, and I knew she didn't just mean that incident, but her entire childhood.

Something about my mother, in that moment, seemed real to me, like it never had before, something vulnerable and pure. I wanted to tell her about a night when I, also eighteen, was attending community college in Jamestown and living apart from her for the first time. Drunk and depressed about my disabilities, I drank Comet cleanser, tied a plastic bag over my head, and lay down on my bed, hoping never to wake up. A friend found me and, thinking it was just some kind of prank, tore the bag from my head and laughed. I wanted to tell my mother how much I hated myself back then, how much I hated my body, but I couldn't bring myself to speak. I knew she'd only blame herself. Instead, I told her how sorry I was to hear that she tried to commit suicide, and that I was glad she didn't succeed.

"There's lots you don't know about your mother," she said,

as if trying to soften the moment.

Then, she went on to tell me the terrible things Nana did to her and my uncle Joe. "You remember that music box in Nana's kitchen?" she asked. "The one you and Aiesha loved?"

I nodded. I knew where this was leading. I'd heard these stories before. After my grandfather had left for work at his second of two full-time jobs (the midnight trick at the steel plant), my nana would pull the string on the music box as my mother and uncle sat huddled at the top of the stairs, she picking her lips, and my uncle his fingers.

"We knew that when the music stopped, she'd come for us," my mother said, and took a long drag off her cigarette. "She was like *Mommie Dearest*."

My mother told me that my uncle always tried to protect her from my nana's wrath, even if that meant risking injury himself. She told me about the time my nana jumped out of the closet and tried to stab my uncle with a kitchen knife, and the time she stuck my mother's favorite doll with hundreds of pins and left it where she knew my mother would find it.

When I'd first heard these stories nearly thirty years earlier, I couldn't reconcile that woman with my nana: the woman who doted on me with her perfumed kisses.

After a moment, my mother told me about my nana's crying fits, fits of uncontrollable laughter, and how my grandfather used to slap her to make her stop. She told me about the weekly enemas my nana forced her and my uncle to endure.

Then, it hit me: it was my grandmother who was chasing my mother those many nights her screaming jolted me from a deep sleep. "No! Stop! Please!" she begged, and I'd run to her, unable to wake her, unable to help her, just as I was unable to help her now. It had been twenty-nine years since my nana died, nearly sixty since my mother took a handful of sleeping pills, yet I could tell by watching her that her wounds were still fresh, and that she relived those events every day in her mind.

When things were bad, my mother always turned to her aunt Rose. Many nights, while my grandfather was at work, my nana, convinced he was out with another woman, made my mother and uncle pack their clothes in a suitcase. Then she dragged them to Rose's house, five blocks away. On one of these occasions my mother's shoulder was dislocated from being pulled down the street. Only when they reached Rose's house was her arm attended to. Rose probably made coffee, set out cookies or donuts, and sent my mother and uncle into another room while she and my nana talked it out. Eventually, after my nana had calmed down, Rose convinced her to go home.

In another incident, after my parents returned from their honeymoon, my mother went to pick up her clothes and found that in her absence, my nana had thrown them all away. "We just stood there in my bedroom," my mother said, "staring at one another. Neither of us spoke a word."

Once, when my mother was six or seven, she came home from school to find my nana in the basement, standing on a chair with a noose around her neck.

"It's because of you!" my nana yelled, pointing at my mother. "It's all your fault." My mother ran up the basement stairs and out the back door to a neighbor's house for help.

I was certain that *this*, more than any other moment, had set the trajectory my mother's life would follow. This was the moment she would forever be running from and returning to.

It's all your fault, my nana had said. Was she really planning on hanging herself? Or was it all a show, like her feigned illnesses? Was this the actress my nana always dreamed of becoming? The performance artist?

"I'm not saying there were never any good times," my mother tried to assure me. "We had lots of fun—Christmas, Easter, trips to New York, Youngstown, Cleveland, Quebec."

Maybe it was just the times. What went on in the house, as my mother said, stayed in the house. Mental illness was something to be ashamed of, the result of some moral failing. The same was said about cancer, birth defects, and alcoholism. Yet I still wondered why no one—my grandfather or aunt Rose—did anything to try to help my nana. If she had gone to a doctor, would they have diagnosed with schizophrenia? Or some other malady? Would she have been institutionalized? Would it have made a difference?

If I were to ask my uncle Joe, he'd scoff and accuse my mother of exaggerating. He'd admit, however, that my nana did pull a knife on him and that she waited with a noose in the basement for my mother. But he'd claim these were isolated incidents. My aunt Stephanie would say how welcoming my nana was, how easy she was to talk to. "She made me feel so welcome. I felt closer to her than my own mother."

Even Aiesha and Amanda had a hard time believing these stories. As for me, I believe both my mother's and uncle's versions. Maybe it was just easier for my uncle to pretend these were just "isolated incidents" scattered amid an otherwise happy childhood. For my mother, however, the mark they left was palpable, and their memory stained everything.

Beyond the Moon & Stars

Tuesday, January 8, 2019

I'd spent the last 90-plus hours in my mother's apartment, watching her deteriorate, listening to horror stories about my nana. I felt I was going mad. I had a bladder infection that at times sent me crumpling to the floor in pain, and if that wasn't enough, my mother had been listening to the song "Beyond the Moon and Stars" on an endless loop on YouTube. *When life's great journey ends, and day is done,* Dan Schutte sang with my mother's straining voice accompanying him, *then may our eyes behold your Holy One.* Jenny would arrive tomorrow, but that was still eighteen hours away. I needed to clear my head. I needed fresh air. I needed a drink, possibly several.

I called my friend Kevin and asked if he'd meet me at Rookie's Sports Bar. We hadn't seen each other in over a decade but kept in touch through Facebook. Back in 1981, around the time my parents were newly divorced, Kevin was 18 or 19. He was a soldier in the U.S. Army stationed in South Korea, near the DMZ. His mother, Mary, asked students at Saint Elizabeth's to be pen pals with him. She said he was lonely so far away from home. I knew some of his brothers, so I decided to write to him, and, to my surprise, he wrote back. We exchanged letters for nearly a year, and then one day, he showed up at our front door dressed in his Army uniform—gold pins blazing. Kevin became the first of my many "big brothers" I'd seek out in my father's absence.

As I zipped my coat, preparing to walk the ten blocks to Rookie's, my mother looked up at me and said, "You'd better tell everyone goodbye," as if I were the one who was dying.

At Rookie's, amid a sea of familiar faces, the jukebox thumped a mix of classic rock and hip-hop. I found Kevin and we claimed two stools at the bar, then ordered drinks: a beer for me, a ginger ale for him. He'd been sober, he reminded me, for nearly as long as it had been since we last saw each other. I told him about my mother, and he talked about his family, about the suicide prevention nonprofit he founded for veterans. After an hour we parted ways, promising to stay in touch, though I doubted we would.

On my walk home, listening to the sound of my boots on the snowy sidewalk, I thought about all the places my mother and I traveled together, places we'd never visit again.

Once, on a whim, when I was thirteen or fourteen, we hopped in our car and drove to Elmira, NY. We stayed the night at a motel, then the next morning drove to Corning. As we stood near the ticket booth of the Corning Glass Museum, my mother realized she didn't have enough money for our admission. Suddenly, she spied two visitor badges lying on the floor.

"Look, Jay," she screamed and pointed. "You dropped our visitor tags!" I rushed to the spot and picked them up. The woman at the ticket booth, watching this entire escapade, said nothing. We clipped the badges to our jackets and entered the museum.

By the time I graduated high school, I'd been experiencing painful kidney and bladder infections for over a year, though I kept it secret, fearing I'd have to be admitted to the hospital. My fear only intensified when my urologist, Dr. Saul Abrams, claimed, without taking any tests, that there was a good chance that I had cancer. My nana had died less than a month earlier and the idea that now I had cancer was too much for my mother.

She scheduled an appointment with Dr. Engel at Johns Hopkins in Baltimore for a second opinion.

It was summer. I'd be starting community college in the fall. Our trip to the Baltimore and Washington, D.C. area would be the first time we actually went on a vacation. Dr. Engel put our fears to rest, assuring me that the problem was not cancer, but a buildup of fluids in my bladder. He suggested I find a urologist in my hometown and get regular bladder irrigations.

With the good news, my mother decided to show me the sights in D.C.—the neighborhoods she had lived and worked in during the mid-60s. Our first stop was the Vietnam Memorial Wall. We found Vinny Rossotto's name among thousands of others. Vinny was my mother's childhood friend Loretta's kid brother. From there we drove by the White House, and the Chamber of Commerce—where my mother once worked. Then we went to Arlington Cemetery and stood at the eternal flame at JFK's grave.

The last time my mother and I went anywhere together was September 2000, when I was twenty-nine and we drove to Boston to see an exhibit of Van Gogh's self-portraits. I'd become obsessed with Van Gogh and read his letters as if they were scripture. My mother loved his sunflowers, *Starry Night*, and *Bedroom in Arles*. In my mind, Van Gogh was a true artist, who lived the way I thought an artist was meant to live—alone and tragically.

After Boston, we visited Walden Pond, Concord, Salem, and the National Shrine of Divine Mercy in Stockbridge, where we walked the path of the life-sized Stations of the Cross.

On our drive home, my mother, behind the wheel, approached a toll booth a few miles east of Buffalo. It was dark. It was raining. Lights from the toll booths and other cars and trucks blurred against the wet pavement. We were about fifty yards away when my mother slammed on the brakes. Traffic swerved around us, horns honking.

"I can't, I can't!" my mother screamed. Once she calmed down, I convinced her to let me drive. On the count of three we jumped out of the car and switched places, and I drove the rest of the way home.

*

Now, nearing the corner of Park Avenue and Fourth Street, I stopped and leaned against the chain link fence that enclosed the courtyard of Saint Elizabeth's school. Looking up, I could see the church spire shining overhead.

Why had I called Kevin? Why not Mike or Vin? The last time we saw each other was in 2003. He and his family had just moved back to the area after years of living in Colorado. I was home from grad school for the summer and read at a benefit for his father, who was in the final stages of brain cancer. Maybe, subconsciously, I thought he'd have some answers, some words of wisdom, even.

It was nearly midnight, but the hands of the church clock were stuck at 5:05. I felt the alcohol swimming in my head, and a chill in my bones. I continued walking. Crossing Fourth Street, the shadow of the Lincoln Arms stood like an obelisk.

Tell everyone goodbye, my mother had told me earlier, as I set out. Did she assume I'd never return? Would I return? What would this town be like without her, I wondered.

Straight Ahead

Wednesday, January 9, 2019

When Jenny arrived, on that cold, gray Wednesday, my bladder infection had worsened. I'd made an appointment with my urologist for Friday, but I'd have to deal with the pain for the next two days. My mother appeared calm, and more concerned about me than her own pain, which I imagined was much worse.

Earlier that day, my uncle Joe and aunt Stephanie came by to tell my mother "Goodbye." I watched as they spoke in awkward whispers, delicately avoiding saying that word—*goodbye*—for fear they'd break down. It would be the last time my mother would see her brother, a brother who protected her every night from my nana, the last time my mother and aunt would sit and talk together, gossiping and laughing over coffee or a glass of wine.

That week some of my mother's friends visited her as well. Jackie brought a stuffed dog that my mother named Stella. Debbie, an ordained minister, brought her acoustic guitar and sang for my mother. When she found out Jenny and I were getting married, Debbie convinced my mother that she should perform the ceremony in my mother's apartment. Ultimately, we decided against this idea. I was thankful my mother wasn't disappointed, and if she was, she didn't make an issue of it.

When my mother's friend Cheryl, whom she hadn't seen or spoken to in over a year, called and offered to visit, my mother told her not to bother and hung up the phone.

"Fuck 'em," my mother said. "If they can't visit me while I'm healthy and alive, I don't want them looking at my body when

I'm dead, crying their fake tears."

It may have seemed harsh, but under the circumstances, it was my mother in all her classic and dramatic honesty. She felt hurt. She was being forced to abandon the apartment she loved and felt safe in, along with the town where she had lived most of her life. She was giving up what she valued most: her independence—even if this independence was, and had been, somewhat of a charade.

My mother always put on a brave front, hiding not only the physical and emotional pain she was in, but also her dire financial situation. Even those closest to her, like my aunt and uncle, didn't realize how bad things had gotten. I would like to include myself in this group of the blissfully ignorant, but in truth, I helped facilitate this facade on many occasions, knowing it was more about my mother's pride than anything else. Maybe I just saw what I wanted to see. Maybe it was the only way I could justify leaving her and going off and living the life I wanted to live, which I did.

Because I was having bladder spasms, I left it to Jenny to load our car with those possessions my mother couldn't live without. We decided to leave the rest of her things and come back at a future date—most likely after my mother died, though this was never spoken aloud.

With each trip down the elevator as Jenny loaded our tiny car, word of my mother's departure spread among the Lincoln Arms' residents. Many of them gathered in the lobby, waiting to see her off.

By early afternoon, we were ready to leave. My mother sat in her transport chair wrapped in the heavy shawl Jenny had given her for Christmas. She looked weathered and forlorn, like a refugee from some long-forgotten country.

In her hands, she clutched a battery-operated smokeless ashtray in a white-knuckle grip. We'd bought her the ashtray after the building went smokeless. However, it only worked if the cigarette remained in the ashtray. It also ate up D batteries at an alarming rate.

"You know," Jenny said, looking at my mother, "you don't need that anymore. You can smoke in our apartment."

My mother's eyes widened in surprise. "Are you sure?" she asked. We weren't crazy about the idea, but we knew she was more likely to get hit by a meteor than to quit smoking.

On the elevator, my mother was silent. When we reached the lobby, we were confronted by those residents who had gathered—all the nosy old folks my mother wanted nothing to do with, as well as the few she occasionally talked to. As we moved toward the front doors, a chorus of "Goodbye, Audrey. We'll miss you!" and "God bless you!" rang out, making my mother's silence even more awkward.

My mother was having none of it. She refused to give those "busy bodies" the satisfaction and never acknowledged their presence. It was as if she had already taken leave of them, along with everything else in her life. Instead, she looked straight ahead, steeling herself against the past and what lay ahead.

My Mother Gets a New Job

1985

Sometime in 1985, when I was in eighth grade, my mother quit her job at U.S. News and was hired as the secretary for the First United Methodist Church. This initially caused my grandparents, especially my nana, some concern. How could my mother, a Catholic, take a job in a Protestant church? Growing up, my mother was taught that even to enter a Protestant church was a mortal sin. Protestants, after all, didn't believe in transubstantiation: that the communion wafer and wine actually turned into the body and blood of Christ. They didn't believe that Mary remained a virgin after Christ's birth. And while Father Menge and Father Doyle preached that salvation did not depend on faith alone, but on doing good works, Protestants were not bound by such things. Then, there was the Bible.

"We never had a Bible in the house growing up," my mother said. And it was true—while Protestants were experts on the scriptures, Catholics entrusted their priests to interpret the word of God.

All of this seemed bewildering to me. Wasn't my father a Protestant? Had they taken issue with him as well? Were Protestants really the enemy? It wasn't as if we were living in Northern Ireland, where, each night on the news, Catholics and Protestants killed each other. It was hard to understand my nana's fears. Yet, as time went by, both she and my grandfather warmed to the idea of my mother working for the Methodist Church. Protestants weren't much of an enemy, anyway.

Pittsburgh Part I

Wednesday, January 9, 2019

On the day we left Dunkirk, my mother rode shotgun. I slouched in the backseat, in pain from bladder spasms, crammed in with all her belongings. It was a stressful day. After driving up from Pittsburgh earlier, Jenny now drove us back. It was cold and windy. My mother, wrapped in her shawl, barely made a sound the entire trip. She didn't even ask to go to the bathroom when we stopped outside Erie.

As we neared the Parkway exit that led to our neighborhood, I called the Edgewood Fire Department. I'd spoken with them the day before and they agreed to help get my mother up the two flights of stairs to our apartment.

Three EMTs and a nurse from hospice met us outside our building. The EMTs lifted my mother out of our car and strapped her to a dolly as if she were Hannibal Lecter. Then, they carried her up the stairs.

Once in our apartment, the EMTs put my mother on our couch. The nurse had forms for us to fill out and started talking about evacuation plans in case of an emergency. I could tell my mother was annoyed.

When my mother announced that she had to go to the bathroom, the nurse asked which one of us would help her. Jenny and I looked at her in confusion. Just hours earlier, in Dunkirk, she was able to stand up on her own and, with the help of her walker, navigate to the bathroom or kitchen on her own. Now, in Pittsburgh, my mother was suddenly unable to do this. She couldn't even get out of our car.

This was an *Oh, Shit!* moment. My mother was really moving in with us, and whether I chose to admit it or not, she was also dying. Neither Jenny nor I were prepared.

Though the nurse seemed put off, she helped my mother to the bathroom.

Then, the EMTs brought my mother into our back room. In the doorway, seeing her multi-colored rug, her books and DVDs, frog figurines, her favorite photos and paintings, my grandfather's rocking chair, and the new hospital bed in the corner, my mother burst into tears.

I felt helpless watching her, like a spectator watching a movie whose ending I somehow already knew.

High School, Alcohol, & the Methodists

1985 – 1987

Thanks to Mrs. Colletti, I graduated eighth grade with honors, earning higher grades those two years under her instruction than I had in all my years at Saint Elizabeth's. In the fall of 1985, I, along with JoJo, Mike, and our seventeen other classmates became freshmen at Dunkirk High School.

I imagined high school would be a great transformation, that I'd become someone different and new, that I'd be popular, and that I'd find a girlfriend. I was wrong.

I did not become popular—not among the mullet-haired stoners, or the jocks who slouched against their lockers before the homeroom bell, and certainly not with girls, who gazed at me with a mix of bemused horror and pity, as if I were some freakish puppy panting for their affection.

I wasn't required to participate in gym class, save for square dancing, so I never changed clothes. Instead, I'd sit in the locker room as my classmates changed into and out of their gym clothes, envious of their bodies, which were free of scars, club feet or ostomies. They were perfect in their normalcy. I could not tell my mother about this, nor about the bullying I endured. I could never "Whoop 'em all" like my father had done. Instead, I acted out. I picked on other kids. I understand now it was a way for me to deflect attention away from my disabilities, a way to hide from the world. Getting drunk was another.

My first encounters with alcohol—at thirteen or fourteen—were nothing short of a revelation, like receiving a holy sacrament. Getting shit-faced drunk not only helped me hide the shame and awkwardness I felt about my disabilities, but it also made me feel invincible, as if somehow, I was not bound by the laws of time, space, or gravity. It soon became a part of my identity. With JoJo at my side, we drank beer, Mad Dog 20/20, whiskey, vodka, rum, and anything else we could get our hands on. It was consumed in garages and playgrounds, and at friends' houses when their parents weren't home. Getting drunk became my ambition, my road to salvation if there was any salvation to be had.

One night, there was a party at JoJo's house. I brought my overnight drainage bag (a bag that connected to my ostomy bag with a long tube). This bag filled up overnight, so I didn't have to wake up every hour or so to empty my ostomy bag. I was now prepared to stay the night, prepared to drink until I passed out. To my horror, when I woke up the next morning, I found that the bag had leaked all over the bed and me as well. Those who also spent the night stared at me in stunned silence. I felt tears welling up in my eyes. I wanted to run, but I was frozen with fear and shame. JoJo told me not to worry. He said it was okay. But of course, it wasn't.

Once word got around about my ostomies, some kids—the very ones I wanted to like me—would come up and punch me in the stomach, knowing my bag would leak and my pants would darken with piss. The only way I could fight back, the only way I felt I could control my life, was to play the clown and act as if I didn't care. I brushed off the name calling: *living abortion, freak, queer.* Instead, in a kind of retaliation, or bravado, I knocked books out of upper classmates' hands as they walked in the halls and made fun of those students I knew were weaker than me, like Ezra, a refugee from Central America, and Tammy, who chased after pennies students threw at her. I'd do anything for a laugh, to feel as if I belonged, though deep down, I knew I didn't.

It was during this time that the monster in the mirror returned. Sometimes it showed up when I least expected, when I was lost in my thoughts, or feeling good about myself, forgetting, for a time, my deformities. The monster appeared in the eyes of strangers as well as my classmates. I saw it reflected in the windows of buildings and cars as I passed: a crooked and bent figure, stunted and grotesque, like a mangled Giacometti sculpture. It appeared as if to remind me, like my grandmother often reminded me, that I was getting too big for my britches.

Ironically, it was the Methodists—those enemies of the one, true faith—who saved me. If high school taught me anything, it was that outside the protection of my family, I was not guaranteed love, or acceptance. I was not considered special. But I felt a sense of belonging in the Methodist Church's youth group. Pastor Irv, my mother's boss, convinced me to join.

My mother and I stopped attending Mass at Saint Elizabeth's. Was it because the church did not grant her an annulment? Did she feel obligated to attend services at the Methodist Church since she worked there? Whatever the reason, we started drifting from the Catholic Church. My mother also stopped visiting inmates at Collins Correctional Facility. She no longer hung out with the Mancusos or Sobkowskis, and I stopped hanging out with Mike and JoJo. It all happened without us noticing it: days turned into weeks, weeks into months, and before we knew it, we'd once again carved out a new life for ourselves.

Pastor Irv and my mother seemed to hit it off immediately. They went shopping together and out to dinner two or three times a week. My mother even became a youth group advisor. Many people thought they were a couple. Irv did, in fact, propose to my mother on more than one occasion. Each time, she replied with an adamant and curt *No!*

Despite my mother's refusal to marry him, Irv became a fixture in our lives for the next twenty years. Monday nights during football season found him in our living room, sitting in a fold-out chair, a few feet from the TV, a can of Pepsi in one hand and a bag of Cool Ranch Doritos in the other. "Rush him! Rush him!" he yelled, nearly as maniacal as my grandfather. We also watched boxing, including the championship fight when Buster Douglas knocked out Mike Tyson live from Tokyo.

Divorced, with two grown children—one in Chicago and one in Jakarta—and a twin brother in Michigan, Irv spent most holidays with us. He wasn't quite a father-figure, or a big brother, but somewhere in between, like an eccentric uncle. He took me out to dinner and bought me books like *The Brothers Karamazov*, *Studs Lonigan*, and the *Collected Works of Shakespeare*. Even my grandparents liked him. He visited and prayed with my nana when she was dying of cancer, officiated my wedding to Leilani, and Aiesha's and Amanda's weddings.

Irv always dressed in black and wore a clerical collar. People often mistook him for a Catholic priest, which he found amusing. He loved to shock people with his witticisms and crude, juvenile humor. He relished in obnoxious public displays of foolery—barking like a dog, stuffing French fries in his nose, and blowing kisses at waitresses who, because of his priestly garb, laughed off what they might otherwise have found offensive. Irv also possessed an intellect that seemed other-worldly. At any given moment he'd pontificate about the Christology of Irenaeus, the title of one of the many theological articles he had published, then rattle off some poem about excrement he'd written in his adolescence.

As the years passed, Irv's public displays grew more frequent, and more offensive and mean. I couldn't understand how my mother tolerated his shenanigans for as long as she did. He was always good to me, but the same cannot be said for how he treated her. The breaking point came one day after I'd grown up and moved to Queens. They were eating lunch at Bob Evans, and got into an argument over homosexuality—which, as my mother told me, Irv vehemently opposed. Irv started screaming at my mother and then walked out, leaving her stranded without her wallet or any way to get home, and that was the end of their friendship.

*

During my sophomore year of high school, I decided to be confirmed a Methodist. My decision, however, had nothing to do with dogma or faith. By fifteen, I'd grown skeptical of religion. But Irv and the youth group made me feel accepted, like I belonged, something I hadn't felt since Catholic school.

When a photograph of the new Methodist confirmands appeared in the local newspaper and Father Menge saw me dressed in a suit and tie standing next to Irv, he called our house in what my mother described as "a holy rage," accusing the two of us of being traitors. Unbeknownst to me, he'd allowed me to attend Saint Elizabeth's tuition-free after my parents' divorce because he knew my mother could not afford it. Now, he was calling to collect that debt. My becoming a Methodist would forever sever our ties to Saint Elizabeth and the Catholic Church. There would be no going back.

With the Methodists, I met Todd Dopler. We shared a love for Led Zeppelin, The Eagles, U2, and getting wasted whenever possible. Todd had piercing methane-blue eyes, spiky black hair, and a face riddled with acne. He, along with his two older sisters, were adopted, and this always caused him pain. Todd was quiet and polite around adults, even unassuming, but away from their company, he transformed into Dr. Jekyll. His schizophrenic energy was mesmerizing. One minute, he'd be quoting Andrew Dice Clay and Jim Morrison, and the next he'd make his eyes bug out and pretend he was Charles Manson, like in the infamous Geraldo Rivera prison interview we both watched over and over on a VHS recording.

My mother felt responsible for Todd the way she sometimes felt responsible for JoJo, or anyone she encountered who she could tell was suffering. Of Todd, she once said: "He just wants to be loved and he doesn't know how to express himself." She listened to his rants and teary-eyed drunken monologues about finding his birth mother, just as she'd listened to inmates in Collins, the furniture delivery man, and the lady who delivered the *Penny Saver,* our neighbor Ronnie, and the many other hurting souls she'd crossed paths with over the years.

One night around 3:00 a.m., my mother and I were awoken by banging on our front door. Through the curtains, we saw flashing red lights. Then we heard Todd's voice yelling at the police. My mother opened the door and there he stood, dressed in his infamous tie-died parachute pants and heavy metal T-shirt. The officer, who stood behind him holding a flashlight, asked my mother if she knew Todd. When she said yes, the officer left, and Todd entered our living room. He'd been out drinking and could barely walk. Thankfully, he made it to our kitchen before puking all over the counter and in the sink.

My mother made a pot of coffee. Then she washed the dishes and cleaned the vomit off the counter. After Todd sobered up, my mother and I drove him home.

Todd always needed to be the life of the party, even if the party was long over and everyone else had passed out or gone home. It was as if his life depended on it, as if the silence was too much to bear.

It was no surprise that we fed off one another like fire and gasoline—two misfits searching for an escape hatch, for love, or something to believe in. Like brothers, we did our best to outdo each other. Who could drink the most? (Todd always won.) Who was funnier? Who was wittier? Who was more tragic? We were inseparable until we weren't.

On Mother's Day, 2000, Aiesha called to tell me that someone had stolen her car during the night. The keys had been stuck in the ignition for over a year, and neither she nor her husband had gotten around to fixing it. So, the doors were never locked.

We would soon find out that the car thief was Todd, and that someone saw him trying to remove the license plates and called the police. He was killed that morning on Lake Shore Drive in a high-speed chase. The car flipped end-over-end before coming to a rest in a stand of trees. The police officer chasing him said he died instantly.

I hadn't seen Todd for six months when he died. The last time was in November of 1999, at Old Main Inn, a bar in Fredonia. We'd met there by chance. It was crowded and there was a band. I knew he was drunk. Not wanting to be too compliant with his self-destruction, I walked out on him.

His life had become a long, downward spiral of drunkenness and petty crimes. He went to rehab and was institutionalized more than once. He lost part of a finger in an industrial accident. At one point he kicked his father in the shin while wearing steel-toed boots and barricaded himself in his parent's basement, until the police talked him out.

I could have easily been in that car with him. And if not that car, then countless others. I was still a heavy drinker, but I'd grown tired of *his* drinking and his lewd behavior. Still, I felt guilty for years, for keeping my distance, for all the times I'd egged him on, for walking out on him at the bar that night. "Come back, you fucker!" he yelled. "Come back!" But I kept walking.

My Brief Stint as a Revolutionary

July 1986

It was the year of Mad Cow, Chernobyl, Iran-Contra, and the Space Shuttle Challenger disaster. Thrust between my father's right-wing rants, my mother's Catholic humanism, and the stories my uncle Joe told of his adventures in New York and Boston, as well as the daily doses of homelessness, war, and corruption I watched on the news, I felt a desperate desire to *be* someone, to do something great and memorable, something that would lift me out of the doldrums of daily life. That *something* was the New Brotherhood of Peace (NBOP for short), an organization I founded with Aiesha. *Organization* might be too strong of a word. After all, Aiesha and I were the only members, save for our foot soldiers: Amanda, who was only eight years old, and my next-door neighbor Robbie, who was ten.

My stint as a revolutionary began innocently one Sunday with Aiesha and me going door-to-door like Jehovah's Witnesses after eating our fill of spaghetti. We picked houses randomly and knocked on doors. When someone answered we flashed them the peace sign and yelled, "Peace, man!" This didn't go over well with the person who answered the door. Some responded with a flurry of pejoratives and even threatened to call the cops.

We eventually wrote a manifesto, condemning those good old American institutions we were up in arms against: the police, the Army, the post office, the Chamber of Commerce. Though I admit, I had no idea what the Chamber of Commerce did. We strategically placed copies of our manifesto in random mailboxes around my house and my grandparents' house.

The day before my fifteenth birthday, Kathy, Robbie's older sister, told me that the police had come to her house. She said they had questioned Robbie about the manifesto, and that they were now looking for me.

Instinctively, I told my mother, knowing that not telling her or lying would only make the situation worse. I also didn't want Aiesha to get into trouble.

"Question you about what?" my mother asked.

"Our manifesto," I replied.

When I explained the New Brotherhood of Peace to my mother and how we stuffed our manifesto in mailboxes, she glared at me suspiciously, grabbed her car keys, and drove me to the police station.

I imagined I'd be finger-printed, booked, and thrown into a dirty cell with some murderer or child molester. Instead, a police officer ushered us into a back room and pointed to two chairs at the far end of a long table. Sitting across from us, he read from a crumpled piece of paper, which I recognized at once. *Fuck the Army*, the officer read, his face turning into a fist. *Fuck the police!* he said, giving me the same cowboy side-eye my father perfected. *Fuck the school boards,* he continued, his voice growing hoarse, as if he were about to cry. *The Chamber of Commerce! The president!* Without looking at her, I could feel my mother's eyes boring into me like screws. At the bottom of the page the officer read the following: *This is a revolution. We're coming for you!*

"What the hell were you thinking?" my mother yelled. I still could not bring myself to meet her eyes.

"So," the officer began, checking his notebook and looking at my mother. "This paper, along with two others, was found in the mailbox belonging to a Miss Wilcox of Grant Avenue." The officer said she was in her eighties and had been in a state of fear for a week, unable to leave her house.

"Wilcox?" I whispered in disbelief. Wasn't she the great-aunt of Janice, one of my first kindergarten girlfriends, who I wooed with my drawing skills and Six Million Dollar Man action figure? I thought for sure she'd died years ago.

"How could you do such a thing?" my mother muttered, her face flush with rage and embarrassment. "I didn't raise you to terrorize old women, did I?"

"Miss Wilcox caught a boy named Robbie," the officer continued. "Robbie told her that a Black man whom he didn't know gave him the paper and instructed him to put it in her mailbox."

For a moment, my mother, the officer, and I, sat in silence. I could hear voices down the hallway, footsteps, someone shouting. Then the officer cleared his throat and said that someone named Aiesha was also involved.

Suddenly, I noticed that I was sweating and that my heart was pounding. I looked at the officer and then at my mother. In one long breath I confessed that it was all my idea, and neither Aiesha nor Robbie was to blame. I said I talked him into putting the notes in the mailbox, and told him that if he got caught, to say a Black man made him do it.

"I'll say one thing," the police officer replied, closing his notebook and capping his pen. "You're lucky yesterday was your 15th birthday and not your 16th. Otherwise, I'd have to book you for harassment and mail fraud, and that's a federal offense."

Obviously, we weren't "coming" for Miss Wilcox, and the only revolution happening was in my warped mind. Yet the thought that I told Robbie to blame a Black man haunted me for years. Where did I come up with such an idea? Was I some kind of sociopath? It's obvious to me now that I instinctively knew somehow to create and blame a Black man. Was it something I learned from TV? Something I'd inherited from my father? Was that the real reason I refused to kiss the little girl with fake legs at Johns Hopkins, all those years ago? How could I claim to love Martin Luther King and Reggie Jackson and turn around and do this?

Years later, I'd turn on CNN to see Susan Smith, a distraught young mother from South Carolina, who claimed that she had been carjacked by a Black man and that her two young sons were in the back seat when he drove away. After nine days, the car was found at the bottom of a lake with her dead boys still inside. Smith would later confess to driving her car into the lake and killing her sons. She'd made up the story of the carjacking. The Black man did not exist.

It was around the time of the Susan Smith arrest, when I was in my early twenties, that I started questioning the story I'd been told about my paternal grandfather's beating at the hands of three unknown Black men in Buffalo in the early 60s. My father, grandmother, and uncle all believed the beating contributed to his death a few years later. In one version of the story, there were three Black men. In another, there were five. In one version my grandfather's car did not stall, he was simply stopped at a red light. My father claimed my grandfather's wallet, which was full of cash, was taken, while my uncle Bud was certain it wasn't. There were no witnesses to the beating, and as far as I knew, no police report was ever filed.

I also found it hard to believe that my grandfather would take a different route through downtown Buffalo when The Skyway and a bypass highway would have made the journey much easier. If he did detour through the city, I surmised he did it with intent. Maybe it was a neighborhood he knew. Maybe he went there to pay off a debt, or to meet a woman. Though I never mentioned any of this to my father, grandmother, or uncle, I concluded that whatever he was doing on that day, whoever he was meeting, it was obvious he didn't want anyone else to find out about it.

Was the non-existent Black man whom I told Robbie to blame the same man who Susan Smith conjured? Was he one of three, or five, Black men that beat my grandfather and left him for dead? The news made Susan Smith out to be the devil incarnate. Maybe I wasn't much different.

On the way home, my mother drove to Miss Wilcox's house and made me apologize. When I returned to the car, my mother slapped me hard across my face. It was the first and only time she'd ever struck me. For the next few days, her silent treatment felt like torture, though I had to admit I deserved it. Yet, despite her anger, my mother never told my grandparents or my father about this incident. She saved me from any further embarrassment. It would remain our secret, one neither of us would speak of again.

If there was one bright spot in that summer, it was the week I spent at Geraldine and Phil's house in Sussex, New Jersey. They treated me as if I were their son, and took me, along with their daughters Melissa and Tracy, who were both in college, to New York City.

In New York, I walked around mouth agape, gawking at the wonder of it all: the immensity, the rush and blur of the subways and taxi cabs, the beautiful women, the bums. I stood gazing up at the Empire State Building, the Twin Towers, and the neon circus of Times Square. I went to Grand Central and stared at the celestial ceiling. I walked down West 4th Street, Saint Mark's, and Mulberry. I bought chocolate for my mother at Ferrara's, a known hangout of gangsters like John Gotti. I stood at the gated entrance to The Dakota, where John Lennon was assassinated. New York City was the place I'd always dreamed of visiting. One day, I promised myself, I'd live there, but in the meantime, I hoped my recent sins would be forgotten when I returned home.

Amputation

1987-88

Dr. Robert Gillespie was the new head of orthopedic surgery at Children's Hospital. Fresh from Glasgow, via Toronto, he was tall and slender and spoke with a heavy brogue. He had bouncy, salt-and-pepper hair that was parted on the left and fell mischievously over one eye. To many, my mother among them, he was dashing and exotic, like an actor who played a doctor on TV—*General Hospital* or *Saint Elsewhere*. I was sixteen that fall day when I first met him. Dr. Weiss, who had been my orthopedic doctor since I was a baby (and who was also the official doctor for the Buffalo Bills) had retired.

I'd been walking with a brace that had a six-inch cork lift attached to the bottom of my left shoe, but it was getting more and more difficult. My hip always hurt, and I had thick calluses on my knee and club foot. On my first, visit Dr. Gillespie ordered X-rays.

"Not only is your left leg six inches shorter than the right," he said, pointing to the X-ray with a pen, "but you have something called hip dysplasia—a dislocated hip." Was I born this way? Did it happen sometime later? Dr. Gillespie couldn't say. Maybe this was the reason Dr. Weiss admitted surprise when I took my first steps. Why hadn't he ever said anything to my mother or me?

"Your femoral head," Dr. Gillespie continued, "the ball-shaped bone that connects the femur to the hipbone, is also missing." Apparently, the cartilage around my hip, which was hardly a hip at all, and my femur were fused together, forming a bond that, so far, had held.

Dr. Gillespie was optimistic that something could be done to help, though replacing my hip, he cautioned, would be too risky. Bone lengthening was also an option: stretching my femur with screws! However, at a follow-up visit, we decided the best plan was to rotate my knee, which bent outwards like an elbow. To do this, Dr. Gillespie would make an incision on the outside of my thigh and cut my femur in half, then rotate it so the knee faced forward. He said he'd use six screws to hold it together while it healed. Then, there was my club foot. Dr. Gillespie suggested a Syme's, or partial foot amputation—a procedure where he'd cut the front part of my foot away, then pull the skin from my heel over and sew it up. In the long run, he said, this would help me to walk with less difficulty and pain. Essentially, I'd be more balanced.

"It will take a lot of work on your part," he said. "Months of therapy." He told my mother and I to go home and think it over, and call when we made a decision.

My surgery was scheduled for December 18, 1987. The night before, with my mother staying a few blocks from the hospital at Ronald McDonald House, I lay in my hospital room watching television when I was overcome with a sudden, and primal fear, like when I saw my naked body in the mirror for the first time, in the back room of a pharmacy, six years earlier. Feeling depressed and sorry for myself, I prayed to God to let me die on the operating table. It would be better than losing my foot, even if it was a club foot.

The following morning, an orderly took me down to the operating room early. My mother and grandparents were there as usual, to kiss me and wish me good luck. Then, the next thing I saw was my father standing over me. He arrived while I was in surgery. I felt dazed and nauseous, and drifted in and out of consciousness. Finally, the anesthesia wore off. Or had it? I felt my left foot, my toes. I looked down and there they were, still attached.

"What happened?" I asked my father. He turned away and my mother appeared and told me the story. I'd been given an antibiotic called Vancomycin to help prevent infection. Apparently, I was allergic to Vancomycin and suffered a cardiac arrest. "Your heart stopped," my mother said as she brushed my cheek with her hand. Thanks to the doctors and nurses, I was brought back.

Had I really died? Lying there, I felt cheated somehow. I didn't see a light at the end of the tunnel. In fact, there was no tunnel at all, nor any angels. Did that mean there was nothing after death but darkness? No heaven, or hell? Was it all a lie?

A few weeks later, I wrote in my journal that I no longer believed in God, at least not the God my mother believed in, an all-knowing, personal God who was concerned with the day-to-day lives of people on earth. I kept this revelation secret. How could I explain this to my mother? Hadn't she always told me I was a child of God? One of his favored?

It would take decades before I considered that maybe my prayers had been answered that night. After all, my heart did stop on the operating table.

The truth was, I was happy to be alive. And despite my doubts, a part of me held on to the belief that there was something out there in the universe, a higher power. Something that gave life a sense of meaning and purpose.

In all the commotion, I'd forgotten about the Ouija board's prophecy. I wouldn't die until the age of forty-one. Sometimes, that anticipation filled me with fear. Sometimes, I doubted it, telling myself it was just a game. Most of the time I forgot about it. Yet, like the monster in the mirror, the Ouija's prophecy burned in my mind.

*

Four months later, to everyone's surprise, I agreed to try the surgery again. My new surgery date was April Fool's Day, 1988.

While my mother and I waited in my hospital room for the orderly to take me to the operating room, I began to regret my decision. Suddenly, angry and sick with fear, I lashed out, blaming my mother for talking me into the surgery. "It's all your fault!" I screamed.

I didn't know then that my nana, nearly forty years earlier, had spit those exact words at my young mother as she held a rope around her own neck, poised to hang herself.

My mother stared at me trembling. I could see that I'd upset her. She told me to take a deep breath and relax. After a moment we both calmed down, and I apologized.

*

In the operating room, I asked Dr. Gillespie if it would hurt afterwards. "Tell me the truth," I said.

"It's gonna hurt like hell," he replied.

Dr. Gillespie was right. The pain was excruciating. It felt as if I had hot liquid sloshing around in my stump, like someone was turning my leg over and over and the hot liquid was rushing up and down. Thankfully, the drugs I was given dulled the pain. They also caused hallucinations, which I enjoyed. In one, a fleet of chocolate babies, like the Luftwaffe, propelled across a blood-red sky.

When the initial pain from the surgery wore off, I felt phantom pain—sharp, stabbing jolts, sometimes throbbing—that would continue sporadically for decades. Sometimes, it felt as if someone was pinching my big toe. Other times, it was my baby toe. Sometimes, I felt pressure at the arch that was no longer there. Once, the pinching sensation in my big toe happened every five seconds for an entire day, and then, it stopped.

During the weeks I spent recovering at home, my friend Todd visited me every day after school. We listened to music and watched movies. When my mother wasn't home, we stole sips from the liquor bottles my father had left behind when he'd moved out nine years earlier.

By the end of May, I was back in school. I had to use a wheelchair until my leg healed enough for me to be fitted with a prosthetic, which occurred a month later. For the first time in my life, my left knee bent the way it was supposed to. Not only could I wear the same size shoes on both feet, but I could wear any kind of shoes I wanted. I no longer needed the left pant legs shortened, or for my grandmother Irwin to sew zippers into them.

My prosthetic leg helped me walk more evenly and without pain. It looked real, and it became a prop of sorts, a shield that protected me, deflecting attention away from my other deformities, like my ostomies. Once, at a party, after having too much to drink, I took a butcher knife and started hacking at my prosthetic leg, as those around me gasped in wondrous horror. I was still playing the role of clown, yet somehow, having a prosthetic leg, I felt more normal than I had in years.

Pittsburgh Part II

Thursday, January 10, 2019

Work was busy. There were patients to check in and patients to check out, follow-up appointments, and tests to be scheduled. Most days, there wasn't time for a lunch break. And then, there was the phone. The urology office received about 50 calls per day, and I was the one who answered them. I felt stressed, and guilty for leaving Jenny to care for my mother, but I thought I'd need my FMLA days at a later time, not now. I still expected my mother to—not improve, exactly, but perk up a little and show some spark of her former self. Thankfully, Jenny updated me with emails and phone calls. Today, a new hospice nurse was scheduled to arrive.

Lots went on today, Jenny's email read. *Hospice nurse today was Tracey, and she was great. She's very knowledgeable and took time to answer all our questions. Also, lots of other stuff happened.*

My mother's blood pressure was high, so Tracey called the doctor, who ordered some medication. My mother had been on four different kinds back in New York but stopped taking them before she moved to Pittsburgh. The doctor also prescribed a steroid, to help with pain and inflammation.

Her other pain pill, Jenny wrote, *should just be taken as needed up to every four hours. She should take it when pain gets to a 2 or 3. Basically, the steroid actually helps treat what causes the pain, while the other just tricks your mind into not feeling pain.*

In addition to Tracey, an aide was scheduled to come once a week to help with bathing. Unlike in Dunkirk, aides would not come every day. Tracey told Jenny that it would only occur in the “active dying” stage: the final phase in the dying process. “Usually, the last three days of life,” Tracey said. During this phase patients are typically unresponsive; their blood pressure drops, their skin changes color and becomes cold to the touch, among other symptoms.

Tracey put us on hospice’s volunteer service list. This meant that volunteers would stay with my mother if Jenny and I needed to run an errand, like grocery shopping or getting the car inspected. We had asked for someone to stay with my mother when we got married, which was in just eight days.

Equipment had also been ordered: a shower apparatus, a nebulizer for breathing treatments, and oxygen.

The oxygen was just for comfort, not a respirator or anything, and probably not needed right now. They have this for all their clients, apparently. I’m going to clean out a closet and we can keep it there. The nebulizer is if she feels congested or short of breath.

Tracey also suggested getting adult diapers as standby. For now, with Jenny’s help, my mother was using the commode. There were also non-medical details to attend to. We’d ordered cable so my mother could watch her favorite shows, and the cable guy was scheduled to arrive. My mother had signed paperwork to donate her body to the University of Buffalo, and asked that we transfer the agreement to the University of Pittsburgh. She also needed to forward her mail, notify the Social Security Office of her new address, and transfer her bank account information to a local branch. I emailed Jenny and said I’d look into it all tomorrow.

It was a lot to take in. I was grateful for Jenny, her love and kindness, and her generosity and willingness to dive in and help my mother in any way needed. As far as hospice, I was happy and relieved at how thorough they seemed, but I found it ironic that everything was provided free of charge—daily nurse visits, an aide, medications, and medical equipment—while before my mother was dying, she was forced to pay hundreds of dollars a month in a Medicaid spend-down program for poorer services.

That night, my mother chose to sleep in our gray armchair, claiming it was more comfortable than the hospital bed. She slept with her stuffed animals Stella the dog, which her friend Jackie had given her, and her own Froggie the frog at her side, all the while fingering her rosary beads and murmuring her prayers.

In her prayers, I heard her ask Jesus to end her suffering. Yet, I told myself that she was content. I felt certain she'd be with us for a few months, maybe longer.

My Mother Goes Back to School

1988

Long before I had any thought of being a writer, my mother was churning out personal essays in the creative writing class she enrolled in at Fredonia State (along with an Intro to Psychology class) in the fall of 1988. Cursillo and Kairos filled my mother with the Holy Spirit, and a love she'd never experienced before, but it was her creative writing class that filled her with a sense of confidence, the same confidence she instilled in me: that I could do anything as long as I believed.

In one essay, my mother wrote about her struggle to gain a marriage annulment from the Catholic Church. In many ways my mother felt betrayed. Despite her years of devotion to the church and volunteering at my school, church doctrine dissuaded her from receiving the sacrament of communion. In the church's eyes, she would remain my father's wife until the end of time, or until one of them died.

Among the requirements for a "dissolution" are "insufficient use of reason," a "defect" in consent, or the failure to consummate. Like everything, annulments cost money—how much I never knew, but it was money my mother didn't have. She also would have had to drive three hours to Rochester for some type of hearing, or tribunal. Did she ask my grandparents for help? The Mancusos? Father Doyle? It's doubtful. All I know is that she was never granted an annulment. I don't know if her case would have qualified, but the unattained annulment became a sensitive subject.

Another essay, which earned my mother an A, began: *Today is the day before my father's 75th birthday and I want to give him something special.*

She wrote about how as a little girl she craved her father's love and approval. She wrote about my grandfather's hands, hands that used to untangle bubble gum from her hair, hands that were now too swollen from gout to open a carton of orange juice. *The twinkle in his eyes has almost disappeared,* she wrote. *[T]hose eyes would twinkle with delight at my smallest accomplishments.* She went on to describe her father during one of my visits, writing that *his eyes seem to be looking through my son into the past, as though he is looking at me when I was a teenager, wondering where the years had gone.*

Finally, my mother chronicled the daily challenges she faced as a single mother taking care of a disabled child. To her surprise, after reading the list of my birth defects, copied no doubt from my mother's little red book, her professor told her that the symptoms sounded like VATER Syndrome. *Vater?* My mother and I laughed, as if it were some kind of joke, thinking of Darth Vader from Star Wars.

This was the 80s, a lifetime before anything and everything would become available on demand through the internet. Thus, we quickly forgot about VATER Syndrome, never imagining it would follow us through the decades. The truth was, we had more immediate things to worry about. I had my club foot amputated, and a series of kidney infections kept me in and out of the hospital. Both my maternal grandparents had cancer; my grandfather recovered, but my nana only got worse. The following spring she would die, eleven days shy of her seventy-first birthday. With that, the demands of life, and the fact that we always needed money, my mother never got the opportunity to continue her education. She dropped out after only one semester, but the essays she wrote were filled with an honesty and vulnerability that made them beautiful.

Without my mother's encouragement, I doubt I'd have the courage to attempt putting pen to paper to write my own stories and poems. Like her, I found solace in music and books. Yet I wouldn't become an obsessive reader until my early twenties. Before that, it was a struggle to get me to read at all. Most of the books I was assigned at school went unread. That's not to say I didn't love the feel of books, holding them in my hands and thumbing through the pages, inhaling their musty scent. I just didn't like reading them. I didn't have the patience. I was restless, too eager for what was next. My mind seemed always elsewhere—on sports and music, the Army, or the girls I told myself I loved.

One of the problems was dyslexia, though neither my mother nor I could recognize that at the time and I was never, to my knowledge, diagnosed. Words and sentences were jumbled. I would read "The boy ran from the dogs" and see "The yob ran from the gods." Or I'd see a word like *bird* and perceive *drib*. *Santa* became *Satan*. On one report card, my teacher wrote that I didn't follow the rules of grammar. Did it have anything to do with my speech problems, my inability to pronounce my THs, or how as a very young child, I couldn't pronounce my own name? Maybe. I also often confused my left with my right. Math was a nightmare as well. Simple addition, subtraction, division, word problems, fractions, and statistics all befuddled and enraged me, unless those stats were tied to sports like Reggie Jackson's .300 batting average during the 1980 season, which I obsessed over. It was the year he hit 41 homeruns and 111 RBIs.

When I did read, it was my mother's books: *The Prophet* by

Kahlil Gibran, Hemingway's *A Farewell to Arms*, and Hannah Hurnard's *Hinds' Feet on High Places*—a work of Christian fiction my mother made me read. I also enjoyed books about John Lennon and the 1960s counterculture, as well as the Dell Yearling biographies on John F. Kennedy and Martin Luther King, Jr. my mother bought me.

Charlie's Monument was another important book of my preteen years. It was a gift from an ancient Mormon couple who used to visit my house when my parents were still together. Every so often, they'd materialize at our front door, like time travelers. Once inside, they sat side-by-side on the loveseat like stone versions of themselves. I never remember them speaking, just sitting there smiling in mute contentment. *Charlie's Monument,* written by Blaine M. Yorgason, was about a boy born with only one arm, badly deformed legs, and a twisted back. Like me, he longed to be like other kids. He dreamed of becoming a man, falling in love with a beautiful woman, and getting married. Like me, Charlie also had a mother who believed in him and loved him more than anything in the world, a mother who told him over and over how special he was, and that God had a plan for him.

A Taste of Freedom

1989

In high school, I was an average student at best. I was lazy and possessed little ambition or enthusiasm to make much of an impression with my teachers. You could sum up my entire high school career with one day in Ms. Hardy's 11th-grade English class. We were reading *The Rime of the Ancient Mariner* aloud. I sat in the back row next to Dennis, one of the classmates I tried to impress with my self-deprecating humor. He talked me into doing my banshee-style pig call. When I let it loose, the room fell quiet. Ms. Hardy stood in front of the class for what felt like an eternity, mouth agape. Years later, Ms. Hardy would invite me to read my poetry to her class. At the time of my pig call, however, the idea that I would be a writer one day was preposterous.

Despite my average academic performance, I graduated in June 1989. It was the year of Tiananmen Square, Tom Petty's *Full Moon Fever,* and the Ayatollah Khomeini's *fatwa* against Salman Rushdie.

My mediocre grades left me with few options. I would never be able to endure working in factories like my father and grandfather had, and I wasn't about to go to a four-year school. I signed up to take the SATs but overslept and never rescheduled. Luckily, I was accepted at Jamestown Community College. Because of my disabilities and how little my mother earned, my tuition and books were paid in full, thanks to state and county grants. I also received a small stipend from Vocational Rehab and worked part-time, as an assistant in the audio recording studio where I took classes from Lauren Turner, a pastor I met while a member of the United Methodist youth group.

That first semester at Jamestown, I shared a basement apartment in a house a mile from campus with a bunch of guys from Dunkirk, including Vin Bradley—my longtime friend who was also the son of Loretta, my mother's best friend in high school. It was a long, drunken party. Still, I managed to earn As and Bs—better than all my high school years. I took remedial English and math, as well as music theory and guitar lessons. I also became an obsessive reader, discovering James Joyce, Emerson, Thoreau, and Nietzsche. In the only creative writing class of my undergraduate career, I wrote a story about my grandparents' house, which was in mourning over my nana's recent death. I also kept a notebook, jotting down quotes from the authors I read, as well as my own musings on politics, God, and my place in the world, which I was still trying to figure out. Outwardly, everything was fine. I was enjoying my classes and partying like any 18-year-old, away from home for the first time, yet inside I felt insecure and frightened.

When I went home to visit my mother, she thought I was depressed. "Why are you sleeping so much?" she'd ask.

Looking back, I understand that I was indeed depressed, but the reason I slept so much had more to do with exhaustion from partying too much. Living with roommates made it even more difficult to hide my disabilities. Getting drunk and acting like a clown were still my go-to strategies to hide my ostomies, though everyone in the house already knew. The only person I was fooling was myself.

Against my wishes, my mother made an appointment for me to see one of the school psychologists. I went to one session and never went back. No matter what the psychologist asked, I told him I was fine, that my mother was mistaken. I had no problems.

How could I explain my insecurities, my self-loathing, or that I desperately wanted to have sex and fantasized about it constantly, but was afraid to expose my deformed body to a woman? How could I admit that one drunken night, I drank a couple of spoonfuls of Comet cleanser mixed with water, and tied a bag over my head, hoping that when I passed out, I wouldn't wake up again?

A month or so later, I met Janet in music theory. She was a flutist with blue eyes and a wave of blonde hair that looked like piped cake icing. I started visiting her in her dorm room. We watched TV, drank beer, and kissed. Sometimes I'd read her passages from *Walden* or *Thus Spake Zarathustra*. Yet each time we met, I was overcome with anxiety and fear. What would I do if she wanted to have sex? What would she say about my ostomies? As fate would have it, and I truly believed it was fate, she confessed that she and her ex-boyfriend had been talking on the phone, and he'd asked her to marry him. Two weeks later, she dropped out of school and moved back home.

When the semester ended my two roommates said they were moving back home to save money. I decided to do the same. I wouldn't admit it, but I was relieved. Even though I was having fun, I missed my mother.

Our Little Secret

1990-1991

During my first semester at Jamestown Community College, I started seeing my father more often. Our relationship improved during the summer I turned sixteen and he taught me how to drive. He seemed to take a new interest in my life, and I was happy about it.

Now that I was living on my own in Jamestown, he decided to forgo any unnecessary contact with my mother and give me the $50-a-week child support directly through a joint bank account that he opened in both our names. I became suspicious when he kept the checks, barring my access to any money without his permission. In a rare act of defiance, my first since trying to flush his shaving cream down the toilet when I was six, I went to the bank and closed out the account.

One day, my father told me that if I wanted to, he could arrange for me to use some of the money from my trust fund early. At the time, I had dreams of becoming a recording engineer. I found a school in Long Island (only an hour's drive from New York City) that offered advanced classes in audio engineering. Though I still loved playing guitar, I'd come to the realization that I was never going to be a rock star like Jimmy Page or Pete Townshend. Audio engineering seemed like the next best thing.

Maybe the trust fund could pay for the tuition. My father told me he'd take care of it. He told me not to worry. He told me not to mention anything to my mother. "It'll be our little secret," he said.

I was skeptical. As far as I knew, I wasn't allowed access to my trust fund until I turned twenty-one, but I wanted to believe he was trying to help, and that he loved me. So, it became our little secret. Ours and his girlfriend Georgette's.

I was sixteen the first time I met Georgette. It was a Sunday in late summer. I know it was a Sunday because my father was driving his Chevy Nova, taking me home after we'd spent the weekend together at my grandmother's house. We were on Route 5, a winding two-lane highway that ran parallel to the lake. Suddenly, he pulled his car across the oncoming lane and parked on the side of the road, facing the wrong way.

"Well, look who it is!" he exclaimed, and as I looked, I saw a woman on roller skates approach the car. She had dark curly hair and was dressed like Linda Ronstadt on the cover of her *Living in the U.S.A.* album: short shorts, striped tube socks, and a blue varsity-style jacket.

I knew instinctively this was a setup, that my father had planned this meeting. This was his way of introducing me to Georgette, whom he never referred to as his girlfriend, even when she and my father moved into the garage on my grandmother's property that they turned into an apartment.

I admit, I liked Georgette. She took an interest in me, in a way my father never had. She talked to me, asked about school. She knew and liked the music I liked: The Who, Led Zeppelin, and Hendrix. One day, not long after our first meeting, she told me that when I got my money, maybe we could all go into business together (me, my father, and her). My money? From my trust fund? What did she know about it?

In early 1990, during my second semester at Jamestown Community College, after I'd moved back home to live with my mother, my father took me to see a lawyer he knew. It was about eight o'clock at night. What kind of hours do lawyers keep, I wondered, but I didn't question him. We walked up a dark stairwell and entered an equally dark office, where a short man with glasses and a receding hairline sat at a desk.

The man, who called my father Rich, said he'd heard a lot about me. Then, he handed me a pen and asked me to sign a form. I felt nervous, but signed the form without questioning him or my father. Back in my father's car, he reminded me about our little secret. "Remember," he said. "Don't mention this to your mother."

The following week my father picked me up and we drove to Buffalo. He said there was more paperwork he needed me to sign.

"You still want to go to that school in New York City, don't you?" he asked.

My money was in two accounts at two separate banks in Buffalo. At the first bank there was no issue. I signed my name at the bottom of the page. I felt as if I were under the spell of some invisible force that guided my hand.

A woman at the second bank told my father that she could not grant his request, saying that what he was trying to do was illegal. My father grew frustrated and began shouting, pointing in my direction.

"If anything happens to him," he screamed, "I don't want his mother to get any of the money!"

If anything happens to me? Did he know something I didn't? Was he expecting me to die?

And why shouldn't my mother get any of the money? Wasn't she the one who took me to all my doctor appointments? The one who slept next to my bed in a foldout cot when I was in the hospital?

In that moment, I should have felt anger. Instead, I was shocked and ashamed of both of us. Ashamed of my father for the words he spoke, for his lying to me, and ashamed of myself, mad at myself for trusting him, for not confronting or questioning him, and for betraying my mother.

Unable to get what he'd come for, my father ushered me out of the bank. It didn't much matter, I'd find out. The damage, though not as bad as it could have been, was done. The papers I signed at the first bank gave my father complete control of the funds. He could withdraw money at any time, no questions asked.

Suddenly, all my fears were coming true, fears that my father, even though he spoiled me during Christmas and my birthday, didn't really love me, fears that he was embarrassed by me and all my deformities.

The following day, in between classes, feeling sick about what I'd done, I called my mother from a payphone and told her what had happened. She was livid. Later that evening, I stood in our kitchen when she called my father on the phone. My body rigid, I felt it burning with fear, just like when I stood at the lawyer's office, at the bank, and the few times I'd gotten got into fights at school. My mother screamed into the phone, then she slammed it down.

"You need to learn how to stand up for yourself," she said, turning to me.

My mother contacted a lawyer in Buffalo and when we met him, I told him how I'd signed the papers, giving my father control of my trust fund, but that I did so, I confirmed, under duress and fear. I said I thought my father was trying to help me, but that after he yelled at the woman at the second bank, I knew that he wasn't. The lawyer assured me that we'd win the case and that I'd get control of the money.

During that time, I visited my grandmother when my father was at work. I felt terrible sneaking around, fearful he'd be at the house, or would show up and I'd be forced to confront him. In September, my grandmother turned 80. I was told about her surprise birthday party after the fact. She showed me photos of the party during one of my visits.

Though my mother maintained that I was present in court the day the judge read his verdict, I have absolutely no memory of it. My father testified that he feared I'd blow the money on guitars or give it away to friends or to my mother. He said that I'd be taken advantage of and swindled. He said I was naive. He said I was ungrateful. Our lawyer claimed that there was missing money—how much, to this day, I don't know. My father admitted withdrawing money from the accounts but assured the judge it was only so he could pay what was due in taxes, though he never produced any receipts.

When it was over, I became the sole owner of both accounts, which, after fifteen years of accumulating interest, was worth $150,000. I was twenty years old. My mother wanted me to pursue a criminal case for the missing money, but I refused. I felt guilty enough and just wanted to move on. I wasn't even sure my father and I would ever speak to one another again.

My Mother and I Fled Like Gypsies

1991 – 1993

My mother and I fled our house in the dark of night, like gypsies. Almost. It wasn't during the night, but it felt like it.

It was the fall of 1991. I was in possession of $150,000, and my mother and I decided to move. Over the years, our house on Main Street—the one she and my father had purchased in 1972—had fallen into disrepair. The roof leaked in both the living room and dining room. The carpet was water-logged in various places and the floorboards underneath had buckled. Every time it rained, or in the winter when the snow melted, my mother and I dragged out all the pots, pans, cups, and bowls from the kitchen cupboards and strategically placed them throughout the house to catch the water. Many nights, we'd fall asleep to the sound of water dripping, and in the mornings, we'd wake to find the cups and bowls overflowing. The faux ceiling tiles crumbled so often that we stopped replacing them. How long did the roof leak? A year? Five? Ten? I can't say for certain.

According to my parents' divorce agreement, my mother and I were allowed to stay in the house until my 21st birthday. Until then, in addition to the $50 a week in child support, my father was responsible for paying the mortgage and taxes, as well as major repairs, including the roof.

Why hadn't he paid for a new roof, instead of using fly-by-nights like Bart's Services? Those patch jobs were only band-aids that never lasted long. Was it because he didn't have the money? Did he not understand the extent of the damage? Or didn't he care?

If the leaky roof and buckled floorboards weren't reason enough to abandon the house, then the flea infestation sealed the deal. We took our dog Benji to the vet regularly. We used creams and shampoos, but nothing helped. The fleas were eating him alive.

When my mother and I moved out, we packed our clothes, pots, pans, dishes, books, records, and my great-grandfather's rocking chair into a U-Haul and left the rest of the furniture behind. It felt liberating, like skipping out on an absentee landlord, or how I felt, ten years earlier, when I convinced a group of friends to help me tear down the bicycle shed my father had left unfinished when he moved out. When my mother found out she was angry, but secretly, I think she was proud.

My mother and I were lucky. A cousin on my maternal grandmother's side was renting out a house she owned on Jackson Street: a tiny two-bedroom, with a screened-in front patio and a large backyard. The year and a half we spent there saved our dog Benji, who recovered from his flea infestation. He would live another five years.

Around this time, my mother quit her job at the Methodist Church and was hired full time as an aide at Saint Vincent's Assisted Living Home, and I bought my first car from Larry Spacc: a used two-door Pontiac Grand Am. Money from my trust fund also bought new furniture. It paid the rent, the utility bills, as well as my medical bills, which the trust was originally intended for. I was no longer covered under my father's insurance, and when I tried to get my own, I was told that because of my pre-existing conditions, it would cost $900 a month. I decided to pay out of pocket.

The following fall, my mother and I found a three-bedroom, ranch-style house at 123 West Fifth Street. It had a finished basement and big front and back yards. My grandfather, always one to speak his mind without any care for decorum, said I was wasting my life away and that I needed to find a job, even though I'd been working part-time at a convenience store. He also took aim at my mother, pointing out all the ways he believed she'd screwed up her life. Yet, when we found the house on Fifth Street, he agreed to put up half the money in cash if I did the same. The price was $54,000. In the end I paid $25,000, and my grandfather paid the rest. My mother and I moved in the week before Thanksgiving 1992.

Our new home became a sanctuary for my mother. Just as she transformed our house on Main Street after my father moved out, she transformed our new house as well. I hadn't seen her this happy since she picked me up from school after her three-night Cursillo retreat, nearly a decade earlier. It was as if she'd shed her skin and become someone new.

As a new homeowner, my mother was free and clear. She had a steady job. She no longer had to worry about rain pouring in through the roof, or the dog dying from fleas. We were finally getting our slice of the American Dream.

We painted the living room and hallway walls a minty Gas-X green, except the wall behind the television, which my mother, inspired by the Home and Garden Network, painted a deep burgundy. We hung curtains, family photos, and paintings. Many nights, I woke at two or three in the morning to find her rearranging the furniture or painting a stool or bench she found at a yard sale. We spent a month refinishing the kitchen cupboards, sanding off the shoe polish brown stain the previous owners put on, giving them a more natural finish that accentuated the woodgrain.

The following summer, at my mother's request, I painted

the shutters and front porch hunter green to match the cottage John Wayne and Maureen O'Hara shared in *The Quiet Man*. With the leftover paint, she instructed me to paint the driveway. Mr. Colicchia, the old man across the street who could be seen day and night pulling weeds from his pristine lawn, stood staring at me with a bemused, slightly irritated frown as I walked up and down the driveway with a roller. In less than a year, the paint had mostly chipped away, and looked as if a flock of pigeons had shit all over the driveway.

My mother bought a large recliner from a church sale that we put in the basement, which became "my space," like a bachelor pad. Life was good. I earned an associate degree in humanities from Jamestown Community College and was working part-time at a convenience store. Yet, it was clear I was going nowhere.

Each day was the same. I worked my shift at the convenience store and, later, went out to the bars while my mother worked the night shift at Saint Vincent's. I grew restless. I knew I needed to do something with my life, but I had no idea what that was.

My grandmother Irwin offered to pay my tuition to SUNY Fredonia if I was accepted into the art department. It wasn't a surprise when my portfolio—sketches and acrylic portraits of Charles Manson, Aleister Crowley, and the Ayatollah Khomeini—were turned down. Maybe I sabotaged my own chances. Maybe I just wasn't talented enough.

I had maintained a close relationship with my grandmother Irwin, even though I hadn't spoken much to my father in over a year. Ultimately, it was my grandmother who got us talking again. "You're all he's got," my grandmother told me on one of my lunchtime visits when my father was at work.

My father and I seemed to pick up where we'd left off, as if the past couple years had never happened. He never mentioned the money, or the lawsuit. He never offered an apology, and neither did I. There would be no mention of the house on Main Street, or the new one on Fifth Street. The Subaru Outback—a car that my father mysteriously began driving after Georgette entered our lives—was gone, and so was Georgette. He never mentioned her name, as if she'd never existed. My grandmother told me she moved out west and married "some old man."

With a past neither of us was willing to acknowledge, our lives moved forward in an awkward vaudeville. I revived my role as the dutiful son, and my father, the taciturn strong-man and protector, though I no longer needed nor sought his protection, or approval.

I could sense something vital had severed between us, something I wasn't even sure I wanted back. We were like two strangers who long ago shared a traumatic experience but otherwise remained strangers. Could my father sense this as well? Did he long for a different kind of relationship?

Sometimes I thought I detected something in his voice, and the silences in between, a lilt maybe, as if he wanted to say more, but couldn't. Or maybe it was all just in my head, something I wanted, or needed to believe.

"What's new?" my father would ask.

"Not much," I'd reply.

It was our way. Maybe it was the only way.

My mother, however, was not so forgiving. She didn't come out and tell me that she disagreed with my decision to try and repair my relationship with my father, but I could tell she was dismayed, if not hurt by it. "Oh well," she'd say. "He is still your father."

*

In the fall of 1993, I decided it was time to make a change in my life. Not dwelling on being rejected by the art department, I enrolled at SUNY Fredonia as a communications major. I thought I might go into radio broadcasting, though if I'm honest, I had no great desire to work in radio. I knew I wasn't going to be an artist, or rock star, or an audio engineer; radio broadcasting was just a way to kill time until my real life began.

Pittsburgh Part III

Friday, January 11, 2019

After suffering through a bladder infection during the whole process of moving my mother to Pittsburgh, I was glad to finally have my bladder flushed Friday morning. That afternoon, I was back at work. It was another busy day with too many patients and too many phone calls. Jenny emailed me the name of a contact person at the Social Security Office and a fax number for me to send a letter telling them that my mother was now living in Pennsylvania. She said that my mother started to call Social Security herself, as well as her bank, but then Tracey, the hospice nurse, arrived along with Dave, the chaplain, and a social worker.

Visit with the social worker and chaplain went pretty well, Jenny's email confirmed. They recommended that my mother add me to her bank account and give me power of attorney. Up to this point, my mother was adamant about making her own decisions. Even after her stroke, she still had all her wits, though there were moments over the past year that caused me to question this. She believed someone had taken over her computer, but of course, it was possible someone *had* hacked her. She thought people were living in the walls of her apartment, but I didn't make an issue of it, thinking maybe her neighbors were just loud. During our visit in September, my mother asked Jenny to make the bed for her. We assumed that she physically couldn't change the sheets, but later she confessed to Jenny that she "just couldn't figure it out." Maybe there were other incidents and signs, and I just chose to ignore them.

The social worker left papers for my mother and me to sign regarding the donation of her body. She also said she'd look into whether my mother needed to sign a new OLST (Orders for Life-Sustaining Treatment) form for Pennsylvania, which basically said that my mother refused any life-saving resuscitation efforts.

The good news was that my mother's blood pressure was better. But, in the end, Tracey's visit proved too much for her.

Went over loads of stuff, Jenny wrote. *I think all the talk about health stuff kind of depressed her.* At one point, as Tracey went over the long list of what could and probably would happen as the cancer progressed, my mother announced that she was going to take a nap and quietly laid her head down on the arm of her chair and closed her eyes.

That evening when I returned from work, I found my mother staring at the floor as if she'd dropped something—her rosary perhaps, or a prayer card.

"What are you looking for?" I asked.

She smiled as if she suddenly understood the ridiculousness of it all. "I thought my head fell off," she said. "I was trying to find it."

O Lost!

1996

In the spring of 1996, I graduated from Fredonia State with a B.S. degree in Communications, then landed a part-time gig at two radio stations—one in Dunkirk, the other in Jamestown. I spent the summer and early fall splicing tape for commercials, broadcasting the feed for high school football games, and making sure the weekly Top 40 country show, which had been pre-recorded, aired. For that, my job was to put the CD in the CD player and press play. Boring! Sometimes I gave the weather forecast. It didn't take long for me to realize that radio wasn't anywhere near where I wanted to be. The problem: I still had no idea where that was.

I hated when people asked me what I planned to do with the rest of my life. I couldn't even tell you my plans for next week. To my boss's dismay, I put in my two-week notice in early September, less than three months from when I started. "I'm going to hitchhike across Ireland," I told him.

I can't say why Ireland took prominence in my imagination, but by my early teens Ireland, or my idea of Ireland, like my idea of New York, became, for me, a *fernweh*, or farsickness—a longing or homesickness for a place I'd never been.

Maybe it began with my love of maps, or that scene in *The Quiet Man,* which was one of my mother's favorite movies, when John Wayne first catches sight of Maureen O'Hara as she's herding sheep. If you asked my family or friends, they might tell you it was my love of Guinness and Old Bushmills, or my fixation with the IRA, whose bombing campaigns in the 1980s dominated the nightly news.

Most likely it was my love of Irish literature. By that time, I'd already read Joyce's *A Portrait of the Artist as A Young Man*, whose protagonist, Stephen Dedalus, I strongly identified with. If not literature, then surely music: The Clancy Brothers, The Chieftains, The Pogues, and U2. After first hearing *Achtung, Baby,* U2 became another guiding voice—like Lennon's and Townshend's—leading me into that uncertain future.

"God forbid something happens to you," my grandmother Irwin cried, when I told her about my plan. "You'll be all alone, and with your health problems!" Of course, my grandfather roared his displeasure, citing again the facts as he saw them: I didn't want to work. All I wanted was to grow my hair long, drink beer, read my books, and go galivanting God knows where. My father, when I told him, said nothing.

My mother, on the other hand, after considering it, suggested that I travel with a friend. I think she understood the trip was important to me, but naturally, like my grandmother, she feared for my safety. I knew, however, that going solo was the only way I could prove—to my family, and more importantly to myself—that I could make it in the world on my own.

I stayed with Phil and Geraldine in New Jersey for a couple days, then took the train to New York. On October 1st, I walked up to the British Airways ticket counter at JFK Airport, looking like a character out of *David Copperfield* or *The Hobbit*, with a scruffy beard that grew in uneven patches, a gray oversized shirt, and khaki cargo pants. I carried a borrowed hiker's backpack, crammed with clothes, ostomy bags, a notebook, a disposable camera, a few maps, and $700 in traveler's checks. Atop my head, I wore a Greek fisherman's cap my mother bought at a church rummage sale (three nights later I'd give the hat to a woman in a pub in Birmingham, in exchange for a French kiss). I also brought a library copy of *Look Homeward, Angel* by Thomas Wolfe, which my friend Eric told me was essential reading. He also told me to bring a notebook and to record everything.

Eric and I first met while I was a student at Jamestown Community College. Eleven years my senior, Eric looked like Bono and dressed like Gregory Peck. He would become my most influential big brother figure. I soon started to emulate his mannerisms and even dressed like him, abandoning the jeans and plaid shirts my father wore for his thrift-store slacks and tattered long-sleeved button-down shirts. Moving in his shadow, I felt important. I felt invincible, like I could do anything.

At the airline counter, I bought a round-trip ticket to London. My flight departed at 11:30 p.m. and touched down at Heathrow Airport the following morning around 10:30. From there, I descended into the Underground, where I boarded a westbound train with the intention of going to Stratford-upon-Avon to see Shakespeare's home, before catching a ferry to Dublin.

I quickly realized that I was on the wrong train, but rather than ask for help, I hung out with three young men, skinheads, who had boarded somewhere along the line. Two sat across from me, the other took a seat across the aisle. They had a sack full of samurai figurines. One of the gentlemen, presumably the leader, boasted that he'd just stolen the figurines. His accent was so thick it was difficult to make out what he was saying. He and his two underlings looked nearly identical: bald, with sharp, aquiline features, dressed in track suits. Then, he pulled out a bottle of Jamaican rum from under his jacket and, after taking a swig, passed the bottle to me.

This went on for a while, the three of us passing the bottle, while their friend across the aisle antagonized another passenger, who was listening to music on headphones.

Suddenly, the man across the aisle pulled the headphones off the other man and punched him in the face. Blood spurted from the man's nose and before I knew it, the conductor was in between them. The two men I shared the rum with sprang to their feet and joined in the brawl. The train stopped in a town called Aylesbury, and the three skinheads were taken off by the police.

Unfortunately for me, Aylesbury, a stronghold of the ancient Britons and a major market town in Anglo-Saxon times, was the train's final stop for the night, and nowhere near Stratford.

I wandered around Aylesbury in search of a place to spend the night, stopping in pubs on my way, all to no avail. Finally, around 10:00 p.m., exhausted and drunk, I stumbled back to the train station. As fate would have it, a sympathetic security guard with a handlebar mustache took pity on me and allowed me to sleep in one of the empty train cars. He even promised a free ticket to Stratford in the morning.

Alone in the train car, with the moonlight pouring through the window, I stretched out across two seats, took out my spiral notebook, and wrote down all that had happened that day. Not since I first picked up a guitar had I felt such a strong sense of purpose, a sense of direction. Could I really become a writer?

Like me, Eugene Gant, the protagonist in *Look Homeward, Angel*, saw himself as the unassuming hero in some ancient tragedy. He also shared a deep, yet complicated bond with his mother, but dreamed of breaking free and living in far-off, exotic cities.

O Lost! he wrote, and I felt those words like a flame burning inside of me. *O lost, and by the wind grieved, ghost, come back again.*

Return of the Native

1996 – 1999

The flood gates had opened. After returning from Ireland and England, with the knowledge that I could survive on my own, all I wanted to do was keep traveling. If I kept traveling, I reasoned, I could stave off that peculiar anguish—born of boredom and self-loathing—that so often took possession of me. If I kept traveling, I could constantly reinvent myself, the way my mother reinvented herself by moving to D.C. and later with Cursillo and Kairos. It sounded a hell of a lot better than looking for a job and settling down to the rest of my life.

Within a few weeks, I finished the first draft (125 handwritten loose-leaf pages) of what I hoped would be a novel based on my recent travels.

I named my protagonist Billy Cripple, a thinly disguised version of myself, and joined a local writers' group. The group was composed of some of my old high school English teachers, including Ms. Hardy, whose class I interrupted with my infamous pig call, and Ms. Andrasik, who would go on to author a book on the history of Dunkirk.

I was nervous about sharing my work, but hoped they'd recognize my genius. I was to be sadly mistaken. They bombarded me with criticism, mostly focused on my grammar, my terrible misuse of the comma, and my excessive adverbs. One woman called the scene with Billy Cripple drinking rum with three hoodlums on a train absurd.

"This," she declared, "could never happen on an English train!"

Not long after that evening, I quit attending. Instead, I continued to revise my novel on my own, certain, despite a head full of doubts, that it was indeed destined for greatness. There must be readers out there, besides my mother, who would find interest in my journey: how, like Stephen Dedalus, I stumbled on the cobbled alleyways of Temple Bar; how I hitchhiked from Dublin to Cork, then on to Tralee, as the rain poured down, drenching me to the bone. Someone must be interested in how I stood atop the jagged cliffs near Slea Head in Dingle, looking down as the waves crashed into the rocks below.

What I longed for, those nights writing into the wee hours, or drinking more than my fill at BJ's while my mother worked the night shift, was adventure. I was tired of being thought of as a "good person." What I longed for was a cataclysm—an earthquake, a flood, a nuclear war, or an angel, someone, or something to pull me from the doldrums of my life.

In December, that cataclysm arrived in the form of Dawn. I'd known Dawn through mutual friends while I was a student at Fredonia State. She'd been living out west and was back in town for a few weeks. I'd see her at BJ's, coffee shops, and parties. Soon we were planning road trips together. First, to Buffalo, then a weekend in Vermont at a Rainbow Gathering. It was completely platonic, but secretly I was smitten. When she asked if I wanted to drive to California with her, I didn't hesitate.

Her plan was to work on an organic farm for a year before going back to school to earn her PhD in Linguistics. Of course, I knew nothing about farming, organic or otherwise, aside from planting a tiny garden for my mother, yet I was all in, no questions asked. She had told me she only wanted to be friends, that she was planning on staying with her boyfriend, a stunt pilot who worked in the movie industry, once we got to Los Angeles, but it didn't matter. I held on to my foolish gambler's hope that on the road, her feelings would change.

Was Dawn my Esmarelda? The promise of a new beginning? Knowing that my mother didn't like Dawn, and afraid she'd feel like I was abandoning her, I made the terrible mistake of not telling her my plans to drive out west until the day before Dawn and I were to leave, in mid-January.

"So?" my mother screamed, her face clenched in a mask of anger she rarely displayed. "You meet this girl and you're just going to leave? You're just going to leave me, after everything I've done for you?"

I tried to assure her that I was not abandoning her, but since I couldn't say when I'd be back, *if* I'd be back, it looked very much like abandonment. That morning, when Dawn backed her pickup truck out of our driveway, my mother stood in the front doorway, staring, the way I imagined she stared at my father when he walked out our kitchen door, carrying our dog Moses like a football.

The trip was a disaster. How could I have expected anything different? Two months later, I flew home with my tail between my legs, licking my wounds, just in time for Aiesha's wedding. Was this the Ouija board's first prediction coming true—that Aiesha would get married and live happily ever after? If so, it also meant that I still had fifteen years, four months, and some change to kill.

To say that my return home was not met with the same joy and embellishments as the Prodigal Son's is an understatement. I was received with caution and another dose of my mother's venomous silence, which I accepted as due punishment. We tiptoed around each other for a week or so. Then we were friends again, and just like my run-in with the police the summer I turned fifteen, Dawn and my ill-fated cross-country trip were never mentioned again.

Outwardly, everything, as my mother liked to say, was all right. I put up a happy, carefree front, but I sulked and drank my days and nights away until they grew into weeks, then months, still without any idea of what I wanted to do with my life. I moved to Rochester, trying once again to live on my own, renting a small, filthy second-floor room with a shared bathroom down the hall. I worked a job through a temp agency, but three months later my car died and I moved back home.

I found a job through another temp agency at the juice factory where my uncle Joe was the personnel manager. My grandfather had pestered him for years to hire me, but my uncle refused, saying I wouldn't be able to handle the work. He was right. Three hours into my first shift, shoveling cranberry slop that shot out the ass end of a rusty machine, I walked out.

My mother suggested I volunteer at the Friendly Kitchen, a local soup kitchen where she once volunteered. "It'll do you good to help people," she said. "Get you out of the house and stop feeling sorry for yourself."

The Friendly Kitchen ended up being a place of refuge. I fell in love with the workers and clients. I ended up staying there for over a year, working five days a week, serving meals, doing dishes, and mopping the floors. Eventually I got a job at a grocery store—Quality Markets. Around this time, I'd also become obsessed with Van Gogh. His letters to his brother Theo filled me with a sense of hope and got me drawing again. I carried a sketch pad and pencils wherever I went, drawing people in bars and coffee shops, as well as the patrons at the Friendly Kitchen.

If I didn't dwell on it, I could almost convince myself that I was happy, and that my disabilities didn't matter. I had my mother, didn't I? I could always turn to her for reassurance and love.

After working on and submitting my novel to publishers for over a year, I declared it a failure. Then, I tried my hand at writing short stories, and in early 1999, two of my short stories were published in a local newspaper supplement. One was about an old Lake Erie fisherman, the other about a woman named Katherine who takes a bus to visit her grandmother's grave and the disabled bus driver who falls in love with her. The editor who accepted my stories was also the Chautauqua County Arts Council director. She suggested I enroll in workshops at the Writers Center at Chautauqua Institute that summer.

As far as I was concerned, Chautauqua Institute might as well have been on another planet. Founded as a Methodist teaching camp in 1874, it was only a 40-minute drive from Dunkirk. Yet, I'd only been there on two occasions, once in the off-season with my mother and Irv, and once to see my cousin Amanda sing in a choir. Chautauqua held no significance for me, but, it would become a stepping stone, propelling me and my writing into a future I could have hardly imagined.

Poetry & Chautauqua

1999 – 2001

Chautauqua Institute was a vibrant gated community of arts and culture, but if you asked my grandmother Irwin, she'd tell you that Chautauqua was a country club where rich and snooty out-of-towners from New York City and Cleveland vacationed during the summer. These were people who had nothing in common with the folks who lived and worked in the area year-round. People like my father, who delivered fish to the Athenium Hotel when he was in high school, and his brother, my uncle Bud, who did landscaping there.

Despite my grandmother's misgivings, and a few of my own, I took the advice of the lady from the arts council who published my short stories and spent a week at Chautauqua during the summer of 1999. What did I have to lose? I got a week off from my job at Quality Markets, paid $250, enrolled in two workshops—one fiction and one poetry—and paid another $450 for a week's stay at the Minster's Union, a boarding house just a few steps from the amphitheater. My room had a bed and a sink, and there was a shared bathroom down the hall.

At Chautauqua, time seemed to have stopped forty or maybe fifty years earlier. It was a strange and beautiful place. Every street looked like a scene out of *Good Housekeeping*, or *Better Homes & Gardens*, a fairy-tale world of brick and cobble stone streets lined with houses and cottages that looked like wedding cakes.

It was exhilarating to have time to write and read, to listen to morning lectures with titles like "Peace is More than the Absence of War" and "The Dangers of Being Nice." I liked watching the ballet troupe rehearse, and eventually, hearing strangers praise my writing.

Over the past couple of years, along with short stories, I'd also been writing poetry. The poems were all terrible, but I felt driven. Dylan Thomas was the first poet who set my heart racing, with lines like, "Time held me green and dying / Though I sang in my chains like the sea." He was like a rock star. I was enthralled by his words, his epic drinking, and his short, tragic life.

I met Gerry at BJ's bar sometime in 1998, through a mutual writer/friend. A poet and professor at Jamestown Community College, Gerry was fourteen years my senior. He not only became another "big brother," but my first poetry mentor.

Always bursting with word play and oddball references, Gerry was a practitioner of the mundane and the absurd. His poems were populated with small woodland creatures, friends and family, and had a mystical domesticity about them. He was kind and generous, and I was a willing acolyte, malleable to his instruction and charm. Many nights, I sat in his basement drinking beer as he read aloud poems by the likes of John Berryman and James Tate. He also told me tales of his Navy days in the Philippines, San Francisco, and Antarctica, where he served a stint as a nighttime DJ for Armed Forces Radio.

He praised my short stories, but my poetry was a different matter. "You don't know poetry from third base," he spat after reading one of my poems. I tried to hide my disappointment with laughter, but felt hurt, knowing deep down that he was right. I had no idea what I was doing. I just did it, the same way I approached most everything—drawing, painting, and the guitar—I ran before I even knew how to walk. It was like playing a game without knowing the rules. I knew I had to prove him wrong.

*

I was hired as a part-time clerk at the Chautauqua bookstore for the 2000 summer season. As an employee, I was given a gate pass for the entire summer. Back at the Minister's Union, I shared a room on the 4th floor with a painter from Kansas who was there on an art scholarship. That summer, I also met Hilda, who also worked at the bookstore, and rented a room one floor below mine.

"It doesn't mean anything," Hilda assured me on one of those late nights I knocked on her door. "It's nothing serious. It never will be."

Hilda was five years older than me and bisexual. According to her, she'd only been with women. She was adamant that this relationship we had, if that's what it was, was to remain our secret, though anyone who knew us, or saw us together—eating dinner, or walking around the grounds—knew otherwise. Keeping it "secret" was fine with me. I was writing poetry and having sex on a regular basis with an older woman who seemed to turn a blind eye to my deformities. What more could I ask for? People like me, who wore diapers until I was ten and pissed in a bag, weren't supposed to think about sex, let alone have it. I also felt embarrassed, not only by our differences in size. Hilda was over six feet tall, while, according to my driver's license, I was five feet tall, having stopped growing at age sixteen. On the pristine grounds of Chautauqua, we stood out like Tom Thumb and Glumdalca.

In one of the poetry workshops I took, the instructor called my poems "working class," though I didn't understand what she meant. I told her I was just writing about my life, about the people I grew up with. That's what young writers were supposed to do, wasn't it? Write what they knew. The instructor told me that if I hadn't read Phillip Levine, I should. Once I did, I fell in love, just as I'd fallen in love with Dylan Thomas, Lorca, and Antonio Machado. Levine's poems, however, spoke to me personally. They felt more vital, more real, more desperate. The people he wrote about were people I knew—plumbers, barbers, convicts, and factory workers; mothers and fathers, grandfathers. They were written in plain language, brimming with pathos.

After the 2000 season, I was hired as a substitute teacher at the Dunkirk public schools. Of course, this thrilled my grandfather, who still believed teachers had the easiest job in the world.

One day in February 2001, I returned home from subbing to find my mother standing at the bathroom sink. She held a towel to her nose. Blood was everywhere: on the sink, the towel, and the floor. Her nose had been bleeding since one o'clock.

"There's nothing to worry about," my mother said. "You're the one who needs to take care of himself, to go to your doctor appointments. And stop drinking so much."

We argued for a good ten minutes before I finally convinced her to let me drive her to the emergency room. After the bleeding stopped, the ER doctor took a blood test and told my mother to make an appointment with an ear, nose, and throat specialist.

My mother saw a specialist a couple of weeks later, who told her that she had a vascular tumor in her nose. An MRI scan was ordered to find out if the tumor was cancerous. I worked myself into such a state of anxiety that I was unable to swallow food and started puking. It was the first time that had happened in nearly fifteen years.

The MRI results showed that the tumor was benign. Yet, it also revealed the presence of a tiny hole at the top of my mother's head, as well as a small calcium deposit in her brain.

"It must be where I dug that tooth out of my head," my mother laughed, as if everyone had teeth growing out of their skulls. When she was in her twenties, she claimed she felt something poking out the top of her head. Instead of going to a doctor, she used her fingernails and dug and dug, until, little by little, she extracted what appeared to be a tooth. Then she poured peroxide on the wound and forgot about it.

Despite there being no evidence of cancer, the doctor suggested my mother have the tumor removed as soon as possible. The problem was that his schedule was booked until May.

While she waited for the surgery, my mother suffered countless bloody noses and headaches. At another doctor's office for a pre-op physical, she was told that the tumor was not in fact a tumor, but a birthmark. The surgery was a success. The tumor, or birthmark, or whatever it was, as well as several small cysts on her chin, were removed without incident. A few weeks later, while driving to a follow-up appointment, she got lost and missed the appointment. The doctor suspected a mini-stroke, and encouraged another round of tests, but my mother blew them off. "I'm fine," she said. "Don't worry about it."

Around this time, I won second place in a county-wide poetry competition, to Gerry's first place. My poem, "Black and Tanned," was based on a night of drinking with Eric and heavily influenced by Dylan Thomas. I received $100 for nine lines of poetry! Despite all my doubts and misgivings, maybe if I worked hard enough, I told myself, maybe I could become a real poet after all.

Pittsburgh Part IV

Monday, January 14, 2019

After five nights of sleeping in the gray armchair, my mother finally agreed to sleep in the hospital bed. She woke up at 2:00 a.m. in terrible pain, but refused to take any hydrocodone. She hadn't taken it, or the steroids and anti-depressants she'd been prescribed, in three nights. Jenny and I were tired of arguing with her, and didn't want to force her to swallow any pills. I decided to call the 24-hour hospice service. The nurse who answered advised me to crush the pills in apple sauce and give it to my mother with a spoon. She also said she'd order a packet of single-dose liquid morphine, which I could squirt into my mother's mouth in emergencies.

When I brought my mother a teaspoon of apple sauce, she took it without question. Then, she told me to open the window so that when she died, her spirit could fly out and go to heaven. After a few minutes, the medication began to work, and my mother grew drowsy.

Tracey arrived around 3 a.m. and stayed for half an hour. When she left, Jenny and I went back to bed.

While I slept, I dreamed that a tiny Pac-Man-like monster started eating holes in the walls and ceiling of our bedroom. It kept chomping and chomping, going from one corner of the room and back again, until there was nothing but darkness. I tried to move my arms and legs. I tried to scream, but it was no use. I felt as if I were dead, as if I were suspended in a starless void.

My Grandfather's Parting Gift

2001 - 2002

I was at Chautauqua, relaxing on one of the Ministers Union's porches, reading a book I pilfered from the bookstore, when my mother called to tell me my grandfather had died. It was July 2, 2001.

That morning, my mother had been standing at her kitchen window after working the midnight shift at Saint Vincent's. She was sipping a cup of day-old microwaved coffee, gazing at her roses and hydrangeas, when a mourning dove perched on the outside sill and stared at her with what she would later describe as "a luminous intensity."

"I knew instantly Grandpa was dead," she told me.

My mother drove to my grandfather's house and pounded on the front and back doors, but he did not answer. She could hear his dog, Harley, barking, running back and forth from one end of the house to another. Then my mother walked across the street to a neighbor's house to call 911.

When the EMTs broke the back door open, they found my grandfather's body lying on the daybed in the living room, where he'd slept since my grandmother had died thirteen years earlier. After the ambulance left, my mother claimed the ghost of her grandfather (my great-grandfather) appeared to her.

"He just stood there on the sidewalk" she said. "Staring at me with those beautiful green eyes of his." She said he looked at her the same way the bird on the windowsill had looked. When she turned and asked Dell, the neighbor whose phone she used to call 911, if she too saw the man, Dell looked at my mother as if she were crazy.

During the last year of my grandfather's life, he suffered from congestive heart failure, which made it difficult for him to breathe, as well as do the things he loved: walking two miles a day, hanging out with his cronies on a bench in front of city hall, bowling, and grocery shopping, though he still managed his twice daily trips to the cemetery to visit my nana's grave and let his dog run free. I tried to visit him a few times a week, but sometimes, I forgot, or pretended to forget, too busy with my own life.

At the funeral home, I sat in a hardback chair outside the room where my grandfather's body lay, for a long time. People watched me—my mother and uncle, my cousins; I knew they were waiting for me to make a move. Finally, I mustered the courage and stood up. The room where the casket stood was filled with flowers. Their scent was nauseating. The first thing I noticed when I knelt down was my grandfather's steelworkers' union pin on the lapel of his suit jacket, and his hands, which seemed so large, like two stones, one on top of the other.

A week after his funeral, the woman who oversaw the Writers Center at Chautauqua told me that week's poetry workshop had not filled up and asked if I wanted to join, free of charge.

Over the past few months, I'd been thinking about going back to school. With my grandfather's death, it seemed like the right time. Gerry had planted the seed of graduate school in my brain, talking about something called an MFA.

On the first day of the workshop, the instructor, K.P., a poet from New York City, passed around a poem titled, "Fatman and a Poolside Weekend," by Gary Soto. Its vernacular and ordinary language reminded me of the poetry of Philip Levine.

K.P. looked like a cross between Ernest Hemingway and a bulldog. His beard, which nearly consumed his entire face, had a white stripe running vertically from the right side of his lip to his neck. To my surprise, he spoke in quiet, measured syllables.

At the end of that first day, K.P. announced to the class that he'd be offering one-on-one conferences for an extra $5 to anyone interested. I decided to take him up on the offer. I could barely conceal my nervousness, but managed to ask if he knew anything about MFAs or grad schools for writing poetry.

"As a matter of fact, I do," he replied. "I teach at Sarah Lawrence, and I'm a recruiter for the MFA program."

"Sarah Lawrence?" I asked. The name meant nothing to me. K.P. immediately put me at ease, telling me about the college and the MFA program. Our conversation lasted another half an hour, and by the time we stood from our respective ends of the leather couch and shook hands, I was beside myself with a sense of possibility.

On Thursday night, as was the custom, the visiting poet gave a reading at the Chautauqua Women's Club. A student was also chosen to read a poem they'd been workshopping that week. K.P., or rather, his fiancée, Carrie, chose my poem "Pocket Knife." It was about my grandfather, who had died two weeks earlier.

I stood in the spacious, wood-paneled room, my head barely rising above the podium, and read to a small crowd of mostly elderly men and women. I was terrified.

"Sitting on the backsteps by the raspberries' rebellion," my voice cracked, "I finger your tobacco-stained Kingston pocketknife / as if it were a magic lamp / that might connect me to you, once more."

The following weekend, when my mother visited, I told her

about meeting K.P., and how I wanted to go to graduate school to study poetry. I told her I wanted to go to Sarah Lawrence, which was close to New York City.

Instead of asking me not to go, which is what I expected, she bragged to her friends that I was going off to graduate school to study poetry, before I'd even applied. She said that if I was happy, then so was she. As with my trip to Ireland, she knew it was something I had to do.

However, by the time I received my acceptance letter in the spring, the world had changed dramatically, thanks to September 11th, 2001. My mother and I had watched the events of 9/11 like some apocalypse action movie on TV. Now, instead of bragging to her friends about my going to study poetry at an Ivy League college, she was full of trepidation. In New York City—a half hour train ride from Sarah Lawrence—machine-gun-carrying National Guardsmen patrolled the subways and a toxic orange haze still hung in the air.

I told her not to worry. I told her I'd be safe. What were the chances of another terrorist attack, anyway?

Also, up until this point, my flights from the nest had been short-lived and cursory, but something told me this would different. This time, I knew I wouldn't be coming back. Maybe, aside from worrying about terrorism, she knew this too.

That spring, in addition to receiving an acceptance letter to Sarah Lawrence, I was also awarded a $750 grant from the Chautauqua County Arts Council. The grant allowed me to take poetry workshops and paid my rent at the Ministers' Union. Instead of working at the bookstore, I was hired as an intern at the Writers' Center. I did administrative work and interviewed visiting authors for a column in the *Chautauqua Daily*.

Meeting K.P. was as life-changing for me as the thirteen-hour surgery that rid me of diapers twenty years earlier. It felt like my grandfather had something to do with it all, like he was giving me permission—his parting gift. Strangely, it all seemed to fit. Every step of my life had brought me to this moment. I'd been the first person in my family to earn a bachelor's degree, and now I would be the first to attend graduate school. My acceptance set my life and my mother's life on a new trajectory.

Pipe Dreams: Bronxville & New York City

2002 – 2004

I used to imagine that wherever I went, my mother had gone before, acting like an emissary, negotiating my passage, talking, pleading with people, making sure that if they didn't love me as much as she loved me, then at least I'd be tolerated. Now, I was preparing for my own amazing journey, to live in a far-off city—to forge a new life, as Joyce wrote at the end of *A Portrait of the Artist as a Young Man,* "in the smithy of my soul."

Outside of the safety and love my mother provided, outside of my hometown, I felt like a fraud. I dreamed of conversations where I spoke my mind on worldly issues, talked with confidence like my uncle Joe, Eric, or my cousin Phil, who was always charming, and could expound on any subject with ease. Yet sometimes, even when among those closest to me, I was gripped with an uncertainty that prevented me from translating those thoughts into anything that resembled coherent speech.

Proving my worth had always been an uphill climb. Beneath my cloak of careless disregard was the constant fear of being called out as the cripple and fraud I knew I was, of being a fuck-up. Was my decision to go to grad school a mistake? Had I gotten carried away with the thrill of it all? Yet despite all my doubts, I also knew that the failure and humiliation of not trying would be far worse and would only prove my nana's prediction correct: that it was all just a pipe dream. For someone like me, going off to grad school to study poetry was extravagant. I really had no reason to escape, but escape is what it felt like.

Before my big move, I broke up with Hilda, though our

breakup dragged on for over a year. We'd been "together" in our "secret" on and off again relationship for the past three years. I imagine my mother, though she never said as much, had hoped Hilda would keep me from venturing off. Maybe she even thought we'd get married. But I wasn't in love.

While George W. Bush and his cronies continued the hunt for Osama bin Laden, I set forth on a journey into an unknown and exciting future. My address for the next two years would be 99 Longvale Avenue, in Bronxville, New York, an affluent suburb fifteen miles north of Midtown Manhattan. My rented room with a private bath down the hall, in the house of a widowed schoolteacher, had canary yellow walls, a yellow comforter on the single bed, and ruffled white curtains that hung over windows that looked out onto a small yard. There was a desk and chair, and a dresser with a mirror, as well as a nightstand and a lamp.

On my first night in Bronxville, I sat in my room and listened to the sound of crickets chirping outside the window. Somehow, I knew that no matter what happened, no matter what lay before me, I'd never live in Dunkirk again. Doing so, I told myself, meant defeat. The following morning, with these thoughts swimming in my mind, I wrote my mother a letter:

It's quite a change for both of us. I still have no idea what I want to do with my life.

The next day, before she could possibly have received my letter, my mother emailed, offering money to pay my credit card bills. I emailed back, telling her I didn't want her to pay my bills.

You make me mad when you won't accept money from me, she wrote, *and all you've done for me.* For my mother, paying her own bills and helping me pay mine was a matter of pride, about being a good mother and always taking care of me. Even with my trust fund, she felt it was her responsibility to support me. She closed her email by telling me about an Elvis CD she bought: *30 #1 Hits!*

*

If you had seen me during those months, you might have mistaken me for Alex P. Keaton's disheveled younger brother—a thirty-one-year-old man the size of a fifth grader, dressed in baggy thrift store clothes, with Band-Aids on three fingers. I was never in awe of Sarah Lawrence's Tudor-style buildings, the vine-covered lattice walkways, or the long list of famous alumni, which included two Beatles' wives. I was just happy to be at a place where I could write and learn about poetry. Being only a 40-minute train ride from New York City was a plus. I'd meet people there who would become lifelong friends, as well as my first wife, Leilani. What I didn't realize was that no matter how far I roamed, I could never escape myself. The new version of me looked a lot like the one I thought I'd left behind in Dunkirk.

Not surprisingly, I fell back on familiar habits. Playing the drunken, tragic artist (à la Kerouac and Van Gogh) who never allowed anyone to get too close. Looking back, maybe I should have used the money in my mutual fund instead of taking out a student loan, a loan I'd be paying on for decades to come, long after the money in my mutual fund ran out. The truth was, I was more concerned with writing good poems, about getting laid, or drunk, than being responsible. I felt more at home at The Spinning Wheel, Bronxville's only dive bar, talking to the bartender with a floating eye about Brendan Behan and the I.R.A. than I did discussing the craft of poetry with my cohorts. Sometimes I wondered if I was in over my head. Was I really a poet, I wondered. Maybe the only reason I'd been accepted was because of K.P.'s influence.

I did, however, manage to hunker down and write and revise a good number of poems, poems that found their way into literary journals (my first publications), and later would comprise my thesis, a chapbook, and my first full-length book. Unable to come to terms with my disabilities, I avoided any mention of them, save for one poem about my esophagus. Instead, I wrote about Dunkirk, the place for so long I dreamed of escaping from.

As for my mother, she was doing fine, or so I believed. Even if there were a problem, I soon discovered she'd keep it to herself, until it was too late to be fixed.

We talked on the phone two or three times a day, telling each other about our lives. My mother told me stories about the residents at the assisted living home where she worked and any local news she thought would interest me. She still enjoyed lounging in her Elvis Room with the music blasting and tending to her flowers and hummingbird feeders. She went out with friends and spent time with my aunt and uncle, as well as Aiesha, who had a newborn baby girl.

I spent the summer after my first year at home, helping my mother with yard work—planting a garden, and painting the picket fence that encircled the front yard. I returned for holidays, and when I needed my bladder flushed. Yet sometimes, I dreaded going home. I couldn't explain why. Maybe it was just selfishness. Maybe I'd gotten too used to my new life in the city and feared that going home, I'd once again be trapped.

Leaving NYC

August 2006

Leilani and I got together in the spring of 2004, a month before I graduated from Sarah Lawrence. She was a first-year fiction writer from Kentucky, via Honolulu, where she was born and had lived until she was seventeen. Once again, I was amazed and humbled that someone could see past my deformities and want to be more than friends.

After graduation, I moved to Astoria with two of my grad school cohorts, and Leilani moved to Brooklyn. I got a part-time tutoring job at an after-school program in the Lower East Side, which was terrible. The students I was supposed to be in charge of (first to eighth graders), had been at school all day and were not interested in doing more schoolwork and because of my short stature, they dismissed anything I said. A year later, Leilani and I moved in together, renting a studio apartment a few subway stops from where I lived in Astoria. Then we got married, and a couple of months later, we moved to Pittsburgh.

It was a big risk, moving away from our friends to a strange city without having jobs, or knowing anyone, but New York was increasingly becoming a detriment to my health. All the walking and climbing up and down subway stairs was doing a number on my body. My hips and legs and back were in constant pain. An orthopedic nurse once told me I had the body of a seventy-year-old. I was thirty-five at the time.

New York may be the greatest city in the world, but it is in no way an accessible one, especially for people with disabilities or mobility issues. Relocating to Pittsburgh turned out to be the right move. It was about halfway between Lexington, Kentucky—where Leilani's mother lived—and Dunkirk. It also had lower rents, and was drivable. Married life wouldn't be what I'd imagined, but in the beginning life was good. Leilani and I were happy, and even though we'd left our grad school friends behind, we found Pittsburgh's many neighborhoods charming and soon found shops and cafes and bookstores that became favorites.

Pittsburgh Part V

Tuesday, January 15, 2019

Jenny's first email arrived at 10:26 a.m.

The home health aide hasn't made it in yet. Your mom's sitting up in bed, smoking and listening to Bob Dylan.

In a second email Jenny told me that the aide and Tracey were both coming around noon. She said she gave my mother some root beer and sat with her for a while listening to music.

In Jenny's third email she told me my mother's shower went well: *She walked very, very slowly to the bathroom.* Tracey told Jenny that Dave, the chaplain, offered to perform a short ceremony at the apartment, so my mother could witness our wedding. We were scheduled to get married at the Wilkinsburg Magistrate's office on Friday. *What if we ask Dave to perform the ceremony the following Monday?* Jenny wrote.

All in all, my mother seemed to be doing okay. I still felt torn about being at work and not being at the apartment to help out, but Jenny assured me she had everything under control. It was hard to believe we'd be married in just three days. As with Leilani before, getting married to Jenny was never anything I imagined I would do. I was almost resigned to the fact that I'd live a monastic life. Yet, it was happening, and even though my mother was dying, I was happy.

Clogged Arteries

2006 – 2007

In 2006, three months after Leilani and I had moved to Pittsburgh, my mother called to tell me she'd been experiencing severe pain in her right leg. "It feels cold and numb," she said.

I had noticed she was walking funny during my last visit, a few weeks earlier, but she assured me it was nothing serious. "I probably just slept wrong, or it's my arthritis or bunions." Now, she said, she could barely walk.

When she finally made an appointment, her doctor found that her pain was not due to arthritis, bunions, or sleeping wrong. It was peripheral artery disease, or clogged arteries. She needed angioplasty—a routine, out-patient procedure where a small incision is made in her right groin. A catheter with a balloon on one end is then fed into her femoral artery up to her heart. The balloon, as it's pumped with air, creates an opening in the artery, where a tiny mesh tube called a stent is placed to keep the artery open so blood can flow freely.

The angioplasty was scheduled for the beginning of January 2007 at the Erie County Medical Center in Buffalo. My uncle Joe sat with me in the lobby while doctors performed the procedure, which they'd told us would take less than an hour. It took three: my mother suffered cardiac arrest.

Unlike my own cardiac arrest, nearly twenty years earlier, my mother was awake when Code Blue was called. Later, she recalled her experience.

"I was floating above my body," she said. "I watched the doctors and nurses scramble to bring me back."

In the recovery room, when my mother's doctor suggested she stay the night for observation, my mother refused. "I'm fucking going home!" she replied.

Almost instantly, the stent in my mother's groin made her feel better. She no longer experienced jolts of pain when she walked. She even had more energy. What worried and confused me in the months that followed was that my mother didn't seem in any hurry to return to work. She'd been on short-term disability, but according to her, the claim to extend the disability was denied over a technicality and she was forced to start the application process over.

I was working temp jobs, some lasting a few days, some a week, or two. I still had money from the trust fund I won from my father, which I used for big expenses. I gave my mother money for bills when I could, when she accepted it, but by the fall of 2007 my trust fund was finally running out.

On June 9, 2007, my mother received a registered letter from Saint Vincent's, informing her that her job had been terminated. She said this was the first such notice, and that she didn't even know her job was in jeopardy. She seemed more upset, however, that she never received a get-well card from her coworkers. Regardless, after fifteen years of devoted service, she was out of a job, via a single letter, from an organization run by the Catholic Church, no less. The only bright spot was her health insurance. It had covered the angioplasty 100%.

Pride forced her to tell people that she simply decided to retire, and I was meant to corroborate her story. To the outside world—everyone except Leilani and me—my mother hadn't been "let go" from the job she loved, she'd retired. Even my aunt and uncle didn't know the truth.

"I wanna enjoy myself," she'd say. "I want to relax and look at my flowers."

Yet beneath my mother's outward nonchalance, a festering depression was gnawing away. Nearing her sixty-fourth birthday, she had few options. One thing was certain—she was not going to pound the pavement looking for a new job. And where would she work anyway? The County Home? Walmart?

My mother took out a home equity loan, which required my signature, since my name was on the deed to the house. She made it clear, however, that I would not be responsible for her debts if anything should happen to her. Once the loan went through, my mother could draw money on credit and use the value of her house as collateral. She insisted on giving Leilani and me $2,000.

"I didn't have money to give you when you got married," she said, "so now I'm giving you something."

I tried to refuse. But there was no saying "No" when my mother had her mind made up.

All her years of low-wage, part-time jobs had taken a toll on her, physically, psychologically, as well as financially. My mother had no savings to see her through her so-called "Golden Years." Instead, she was awarded a small, monthly pension of $157. Even with Social Security, this was not enough for her to survive on.

The Dead Return

2008 – 2009

Living in Pittsburgh, only a three-hour drive from Dunkirk, I was able to visit my mother more often. I usually made monthly trips, leaving on Friday after work, if I was working, and returning on Sunday. Sometimes Leilani came with me, but mostly I made the trip alone.

I enjoyed these quiet, solitary drives. It gave me time to hash out the thoughts that swirled in my head, as well as poems in progress. The stress of my mother being let go from her job, her recent health problems, and her looming financial crisis, which she only revealed to me in small doses, began to take its toll. She was depressed, and skipped family gatherings. She slept more and more. The stress also began to worm its way into my marriage.

Maybe living within a day's drive of our mothers was a mistake. Both were forthright and demanding. They were also jealous when we visited the other, making holidays complicated. Leilani and her mother often argued about things I felt were of little importance. I blamed her mother for always making Leilani upset and anxious. If I am honest, however, I admit I did nothing to soothe the tension, nor did I make an attempt to enjoy those times I spent in her mother's company.

Once, while we were in Dunkirk, Leilani got a call from her mother. This is the conversation as Leilani related it to me:

"I just called to tell you goodbye," her mother said. "I had a vision that I'm going to die today."

Yet, Leilani said, she sounded happy. She was planning on

driving to the Cincinnati Museum of Art with a friend.

"I left a note under your brother's pillow," Leilani's mother continued, "telling him goodbye." Then she hung up.

Not surprisingly, Leilani was extremely upset and became hysterical. She tried calling back several times but never got an answer (she would find out, several hours later, that her mother did not die).

As for my own mother, she disliked it when she thought we spent more time with Leilani's mother than with her. One year, she forgot we had spent the previous Christmas with her "So, you're not going to be here for Christmas?" she asked. "You're going to Kentucky again? You hardly ever visit!"

Around this time, the transmission in my mother's car died. In the past, my grandfather had always bought cars for her, but he'd been dead for six years. I couldn't afford to buy her a car, not even a used one.

When Leilani and I bought a brand-new Toyota hatchback (after our clunker of a minivan broke down for the last time), I felt guilty. Neither of my parents ever had a brand-new car. But I didn't argue with Leilani. I wanted to make her happy. Besides, the car was in her name. I wasn't even sure if I could own a car because I was receiving monthly disability payments and Medicaid at the time.

Without a car, my mother became a prisoner in her own home, spending her days and nights in the company of Moriah, the dog we got from an animal shelter after my dog Benji was put to sleep the day before my twenty-fourth birthday. She was dependent on friends, my aunt, or—when I visited—me to take her grocery shopping, get her hair cut, go to the Seneca reservation to buy cigarettes, or simply go for a ride. It shouldn't have been a surprise then, that her thoughts would run wild.

She spent her time rehashing all the things that had gone wrong in her life—those things my grandfather was always happy to point out—like how she spent money she didn't have and would always turn to him when she needed bailing out.

The truth was, my mother had done everything right, at least everything in her limited power. No, it wasn't enough. It would never be enough, just as my giving her money—sporadically, as I was able—would never be enough. Was it her fault, or simply the inevitable outcome of a system that forced single mothers with handicapped children to work dead-end jobs and beg the state for help to make ends meet? The myth of the American Dream, the idea that if you work hard enough, you'll succeed and that you'll reap all you've sown is just that—a myth, but one my mother believed.

Sleepless nights found her wandering from room to room, smoking cigarettes and drinking coffee until the sun brightened the sky. It was during those insomniac nights that the dead returned, but this time they had not come, like the ghost of my great-grandmother, to comfort my mother. This time, they came to torment her, to make her feel she was going mad, that she was doomed. She came to believe that she was a failure and that everything that went wrong in her life was her fault.

Some days my mother would call me in a panic, saying she'd heard footsteps and voices in the hallway. She said she woke up in the morning to find the furniture had been moved—a vase, an ashtray, even the couch. She confessed that she sometimes stayed awake all night, sitting in the Elvis Room, because she was afraid to go to sleep, afraid to go into her bedroom. She told me she believed the family photos she'd hung on the walls had summoned evil spirits.

One morning, my mother claimed she found human feces

on the kitchen wall. She told me she feared she was losing her mind. She told me my aunt Nell, one of my nana's older sisters, came to her in a dream. "She was all dressed in black," my mother said, "and she didn't have eyes."

Another time, sitting at her kitchen table, my mother said that she suddenly started sobbing and couldn't stop. Then, she started screaming "Sister Mary" over and over, like a prayer. "It was as if I were possessed," she said.

These things only happened when she was in the house by herself, never when I, or anyone else visited. The only time I ever experienced anything "paranormal" happened seven years earlier when my friend Todd died, after stealing Aiesha's car and crashing it in a high-speed chase with the police.

My mother and I had driven out to the crash site and when we returned home, strange things began to happen in our house: lights turned on and off and a wind-up music box played on its own. My mother was convinced Todd's spirit had followed us home.

My mother's friend Jeanette said that sometimes, when a person dies suddenly and violently, their spirit is confused and afraid. "They don't understand that they are no longer alive," she said. "They need someone to tell them."

The night after Todd's funeral, I lay in bed unable to sleep. Suddenly, I felt a weight press at the foot of my bed, as if someone had sat down. I lay awake, afraid to move. Around dawn, I felt the weight lessen. I was convinced it was Todd, come to tell me goodbye.

*

My mother's sobbing fit and uncontrollable screaming of

"Sister Mary" sounded like the stories I'd heard about my nana, who suffered from crying and laughing fits. My grandfather, my mother told me, used to slap her across the face to make her stop. I didn't remind my mother of Nana's episodes, fearing it would only upset her, and truthfully, I didn't know what to do to help her.

After the Sister Mary incident, my mother got the idea that she did in fact have an actual sister out there somewhere.

"Maybe Nana had a baby and gave it up for adoption," she said.

When my mother found out that my nana had lived in Youngstown, Ohio for a short time before she married my grandfather, she became convinced Nana had been sent to Saint Elizabeth's Home for Unwed Mothers and gave birth to a daughter. She began studying my grandparents' wedding photos, noting that the wedding took place on a Tuesday—an unusual day for a wedding, and that my nana held a bouquet of flowers over her stomach in all the photos. To my mother, this proved she was hiding a pregnancy.

At a rummage sale at the Methodist Church, my mother met a woman she didn't know, but thought might be her long-lost sister. A few days later, at Gerald's prodding, she found the woman's phone number and called her. Understandably, the woman was shocked and outraged, and threatened to call the police if my mother ever bothered her again.

Haunted House

2009 – 2010

One morning in 2009, my mother called in a panic. She was lying in bed when she heard footsteps racing up the basement stairs. "Whoever it was," she said, "when they reached the top, they opened the back door and ran out." She lay in bed for nearly an hour, paralyzed with fear. Even her dog, Moriah, pricked her ears as if she heard it too.

A day or so later my mother called the rectory at Saint Elizabeth's. Even though she hadn't attended Mass in over twenty years, she asked to speak with a priest. Father Dennis, who had been there since I was in school, agreed to come over.

During his visit, my mother spilled her guts. She told him about losing her job, her insomnia, the whispering voices she heard, and how she feared that the family photos on the wall were conjuring evil spirits. She told Father Dennis how she heard someone running up the basement stairs and out the back door. She even told him about the day she returned home from school to find her mother standing on a chair in the basement with a noose around her neck.

After she unloaded this to Father Dennis, the two of them sat a long while in silence.

When Father Dennis finally spoke, he told my mother that the person she heard running up the stairs was her younger self. "It's you, and you're still running," he said. Before leaving, Father Dennis told my mother she had to not only forgive her mother, but herself as well.

On Easter 2009, at my mother's invitation, the Chautauqua

Paranormal Society set up shop in her living room. Leilani, Aiesha, her friend Melissa, and I were all present as the three-man team of ghost hunters set up an array of audio and video equipment, ready to record any unusual or otherworldly activity. They moved from room to room with a machine that looked like a Geiger counter while the five of us sat in the Elvis Room in rapt anticipation of what it might reveal. Two hours later, they were finished.

Days went by. When the paranormal people emailed my mother to schedule a time to go over their findings, my mother decided she didn't want to know what they had found. "It's just too much," she said. "I don't want to know."

I couldn't believe it. Wasn't she curious? Instead, my mother asked for their advice on the best way to get rid of the unwanted spirits. *Go from room to room*, they replied. *Tell the spirits they're not welcome in your home. Tell them you want them to leave.*

When this didn't work, my mother contacted a well-known psychic she'd met years earlier at Lily Dale, a spiritualist and healing community, ten miles south of Dunkirk.

When he came to her house, he walked through all the rooms, as if searching for what could not be seen. He claimed that my nana's spirit was locked in the closet of what used to be my bedroom.

"When she was a child," he told my mother, "she was locked in a closet as punishment."

He also claimed there was a spirit named Jerry living in the basement—a soldier during the Civil War. The weirdest thing he said was that the ghost of my father's father was in my mother's bedroom. My mother had never even met my paternal grandfather. He'd died before my parents even met.

"He's standing over your bed, watching over you," the

psychic said. "He has a wound on his stomach, like he's been stabbed."

The psychic suggested my mother burn sage and take down all the old family photos as well as all the mirrors. "Mirrors," he emphasized, "are portals to the spirit world."

My mother did as he instructed, but the footsteps and voices continued to torment her. She still had trouble sleeping and her paranoia and depression worsened. Soon, she was convinced that someone in California was hacking into her computer.

"Every morning when I turn on the computer, the clock is set three hours behind!" she exclaimed. Fearing the hacker was watching her, my mother placed a band-aid over the laptop's camera.

By this time, I worried she was headed for a nervous breakdown. Nothing I did or said seemed to help. When I visited, we'd go out to dinner, or to thrift stores like we had done before I moved away, but this was like the band-aid on her computer. It covered a wound that was deeper than I could imagine, or my mother was willing to admit. We both had a talent for not seeing what was right there in front of us.

Pittsburgh Part VI

Wednesday, January 16, 2019

"I can't sit up anymore," my mother said, as she lay on the hospital bed. I held a straw to her parted lips so she could sip from a cup of orange juice. When she finished, I wiped her lips and set the cup and straw on the tray. When I turned to face her again she was asleep.

It was 1:00 a.m. The window was slightly open, and I could feel the cold winter air seeping in. It was dark outside. There was no moon in sight, no stars. No lights from neighbors' windows, save a frosted bathroom window two houses away.

Later, I woke to find my mother not only sitting up—legs hanging off the side of the bed—but smoking a cigarette. Her hair, Medusa-like, reached out in an unkempt tangle of snakes. Her face was gray and cracked, her eyelids sagging.

"I thought you couldn't sit up?" I said, confused. My mother just shrugged and kept smoking.

After a few minutes, she told me how happy she was to be in Pittsburgh, with Jenny and me. She told me I was a good man, and that I'd made her life complete. I turned away, embarrassed.

How foolish and absurd I felt. I thought of her favorite Elvis song, "Love Me Tender," and wondered what I ever did to make her life feel complete, being such a heavy burden from the start.

You're a good man, she said. Was I? Did she think I was good those times I told her, as a child, I didn't love her? Or that time she crocheted a sweater I refused to wear, telling her it looked Amish? Did my mother think I was good when I begged her for money I knew she didn't have to buy a suede fringe jacket—the kind Jackie Earle Haley wore in *The Bad News Bears*? It was the summer after I had my foot amputated. I'd just turned seventeen. My nana was dying of cancer, and my mother was helping to take care of her.

Once I bought the fringe jacket, I could never find the courage to wear it outside the house. It didn't feel authentic. It didn't feel like me. Years later, unbeknownst to my mother, I donated it to the Salvation Army.

I can't just pick up and go whenever I want, she once told me, and I knew she was right. All my life, despite my disabilities and illnesses, I did as I pleased, with little thought to how my actions affected the people around me.

As I watched my mother smoke, I was reminded of how often I spurned her advice, doing the exact opposite of what she'd hoped—traipsing through Ireland on my own, driving cross-country with a woman I hardly knew, or choosing to attend a school near New York City instead of somewhere closer, like Buffalo. I knew she wanted what was best for me, but she also wanted me close. Were my decisions made out of spite? Was I just being contrary? Did I know in some way that whatever I did, she'd forgive me in the end?

Money & Poetry

2007-2011

Around the time my mother brought a psychic into her house in hopes of banishing the evil spirits that tormented her, I began receiving calls from her credit card companies—including Care Credit, a service for incidental medical expenses, including pet care.

This was in my name because my mother's credit was so bad. She asked me to sign up so she could pay for her dog Moriah's veterinarian bills. Moriah had tumors in her hind legs and stomach. I don't know why my mother didn't use this service for herself, being desperately in need of dentures. She still wore the temporary plate she'd been given after having all her top teeth pulled twenty-five years earlier.

When I told her about the calls and asked her if she needed money, she told me not to worry about it. "I'm fine," she said. "Worry about you and Leilani."

The following year, in September 2011, I received a letter from my mother's friend Larry. Larry was a member of the Methodist Church and worked at Saint Vincent's with my mother.

I just wanted to make sure you knew that I paid for your mother's property and school taxes, Larry wrote. He went on to tell me how worried he was about my mother. *She can't afford to stay in that house. You must convince her to sell it.*

To say I was shocked was an understatement. Somehow, I'd believed that—despite losing her job four years earlier—my mother was okay. I'd helped pay her taxes the previous year, thinking it was a one-off thing, that she'd gotten behind, but now she was doing better. I accepted this narrative, but of course, I knew deep down that this was not entirely true. How could it be?

I would soon learn that my mother owed $3,000 in back taxes, which caused the bank to put a lien on her house, and that she had over $20,000 in credit card debt. She'd been using credit cards, she admitted, to pay for groceries and health insurance since she'd lost her job. COBRA Insurance, which she had for over a year (until she turned 65 and was eligible for Medicare) cost $600 a month.

When I finally confronted my mother about Larry's letter, she became defensive.

The next day, she emailed me to tell me that she didn't want my help anymore. I suggested we ask Gerald for help. My mother screamed and threatened never to speak to me again. What I didn't know was that Gerald had also paid my mother's taxes a few years back, as had my aunt and uncle.

Here is the deal, she wrote, *I will not tell u any of my problems again, they are my problems not yours. Whatever happens will happen. Whatever is in store for me I will accept on my own.*

I decided to call my mother's bluff, and contacted Gerald, who immediately agreed to pay her taxes. The problem was the next year's taxes and all the years to come.

We all imagine that when we grow up, we'll be able to take care of our loved ones, that we'll be able to fix things, to make everything okay. But sometimes we can't. I gave my mother money when I could afford it. Sometimes she would accept $50 or $100 without a putting up a fight, but we both knew it was nowhere near enough.

I wrote to local, state, and federal senators and congressmen, hoping they knew of programs that could help keep my mother in her home. I even wrote Oprah, but all my efforts were in vain. It became clear that she would have to either sell or abandon her house.

Not everything during those years was doom and gloom. I finally got a full-time job with health insurance, working in the student records department at the Pittsburgh Job Corps, and in late 2007, I won The Transcontinental Poetry Prize for my first book, *Watering the Dead,* which began as my thesis at Sarah Lawrence. It was a collection of poems about growing up in small-town America. Having a book didn't change my life the way I'd dreamed it would. It didn't make the *NY Times* best seller list and neither NPR nor Charlie Rose contacted me for an interview, but I was the author of a collection of poetry, nonetheless.

Sepsis & Marriage

2008 – 2012

During this time, I was dealing with my own health issues. My esophagus started constricting again. Sometimes, it got so bad that I couldn't even swallow water. I was also hospitalized on three different occasions for bowel blockages. Then, in October of 2008, I was diagnosed with a urinary tract infection. My primary doctor prescribed antibiotics and I was sent home.

Back home, sitting on the couch, I saw one of Leilani's Halloween decorations, a little ceramic jack-o-lantern, start to glow and move. Then, other things started to appear and move, things that I knew weren't really there: little animals like paper cut-outs and skulls danced in front of me. I had a fever; my heart was racing. Leilani drove me to the hospital. While waiting in the ER, my hallucinations continued: besides the tiny skulls and animals, I saw mysterious figures moving on the blank TV screen. My fever was 104 and my heart pounded like a mallet against my ribcage. I was certain I was dying. Leilani called my mother and two days later, with my condition not improving, my uncle Joe and aunt Stephanie drove my mother down to Pittsburgh.

Outside my room, my mother saw a poster about sepsis and mentioned the possibility that I might have it to my nurses and doctors. After that, they changed my medication and I started to improve. Once again, my mother saved me.

If all this wasn't enough, Leilani and I were trying to adopt a child. Our trying to adopt never actually got further than the "talking about it" stage, though we did buy baby socks, a rattle, and a blanket, and tucked them away in a bottom drawer, as if somehow a baby would magically appear.

Looking back, I'm sure this was an attempt to hold our crumbling marriage together. I'm embarrassed by the person I'd become in those years. I took my insecurities and anger over my disabilities out on Leilani and was insensitive to her own needs and fears. It seemed like we were always arguing. I'd yell, and she'd cry. She'd cry about her job, about the arguments she'd had with her mother, or about being afraid—afraid of the neighbors, of driving, the ice on the sidewalk, or being left alone.

The breaking point would come when I refused to go on vacation. I felt guilty about spending money on something that wasn't needed when my mother couldn't even afford to pay her taxes. In the end, Leilani spent a week at her mother's, while I remained in Pittsburgh.

Ten months later, in June 2012, Leilani told me she wanted to see other people.

In August, we agreed to separate, and I moved into an efficiency apartment. We attended a few counseling sessions, but when the counselor suggested I "go out and get laid," I quit going. It was all a shock that sent me into a depression, yet, as Leilani later pointed out, during one of the three counseling sessions we went to, "You never really fought for us to get back together."

During one of my visits home, I unloaded everything on my mother. She calmly told me how, for the past couple years, I always seemed on edge. Up until that moment, I hadn't realized how unhappy I had become.

VATER Syndrome

2011

On a Saturday in March of 2011, my mother called to tell me about a document she found. She sounded ecstatic. I couldn't tell if she was crying or laughing. "I was looking through some old papers in the basement," she said. "I found a letter from Johns Hopkins." The letter was a discharge summary from Doctor Thomas Howard, dated December 2, 1973. My mother said she didn't remember Doctor Howard, but the letter detailed tests I'd undergone, as well as my overall condition at the time: "First of all," my mother's voice sharp and high in my ear read, "the child has multiple congenital anomalies, and it was the opinion of one genetics consultant that this child has the VATER association."

VATER? Wasn't that what my mother's creative writing instructor said over twenty years ago, after reading her essay about caring for a child with disabilities? Didn't we laugh about it at the time, thinking of Darth Vader? Hadn't my parents always believed my birth defects were caused by X-rays?

After we hung up, I emailed Doctor Engel, who performed my urostomy in 1981, and asked him if he remembered anything about VATER or if it was even a possibility. Thanks to the internet we were still in touch. He had even published a goofy poem I wrote called "Hors d'oeuvres at the Urology Museum," when he was curator of the William P. Didusch Museum of the American Urological Association. Now retired, he and his wife lived in Key West.

In an email dated March 3, 2011, Doctor Engel replied: *I*

cannot remember what specific problems you had then, but if my memory doesn't play tricks on me, you may very well have VATER association. We do not know the cause of this, and assume it is due to a genetic defect. Radiation has been looked at, but I believe it is not an accepted cause. So, your mother is in the clear.

Your mother is in the clear! What an amazing sentence. After reading the email I immediately called my mother. She had always believed my birth defects were her fault for having the X-rays after the car accident. It had, in a way, become a part of her, as it had become for me as well as my father, a narrative of our lives we'd come to accept. But after carrying that guilt for 40 years, it wasn't easy to let it go. I don't know if my mother ever stopped blaming herself.

When I told my father about Doctor Engel's email and handed him a stack of pages about VATER Syndrome that I'd printed off the internet, he looked at me dumbfounded and shrugged his shoulders. Maybe it was too much for him to take in. He'd also blamed my mother for my birth defects, and like her, he wasn't about to put the past behind him so easily.

At the time, I didn't know a great deal about VATER Syndrome, but have since done research. According to the Cleveland Clinic's webpage, VATER Syndrome, also known as VACTERL Association, is a complex condition that affects several parts of the body including the vertebrae, anus, heart, trachea, esophagus, kidney, and limbs. VATER happens in approximately 1 in 10,000 to 1 in 40,000 births. I had all the variations and abnormalities associated with the syndrome—how lucky. Though it's not hereditary (it usually only affects one person in a family), genetic and environmental factors can determine who may be at risk as well as the severity of the symptoms.

Even though I'd encountered countless kids in the hospital

over the years with various medical conditions, a part of me still believed I was an anomaly, that God, if he existed, had it out for me. I was the only handicapped or disabled kid in my school until I met Joanie, in junior high. Joanie, like her older sister, had muscular dystrophy. Then, when I was fifteen, I met Charlie, the only other person I knew with ostomies.

We shared the same doctors at Children's Hospital. He stayed a week at my house one summer and my mother even changed his ostomy bags. We kept in touch for many years, but lost touch in the early 2000s. Charlie died in 2005. There were also the kids my mother taught in vacation bible school—their twisted bodies frozen like misshaped trees—they would always be in need, in ways I was not. Seeing them made me feel grateful for my life, though at times I still believed I was doomed, that no one else felt the pain I felt.

After Doctor Engel's email, I found a VATER support group on Facebook. There were close to 400 members from around the world, and many were in Pittsburgh. They talked about ongoing surgeries and financial problems, and I was forced, at age 40, to take stock of my life, and admit that my life wasn't as terrible as I sometimes believed.

Through Facebook, I also found a couple of local support groups for specific health problems. At one meeting, I listened to a man who was a double above-the-knee amputee talk about a cruise he and his wife went on, all the preparations they made and the different stump socks he had for various climates and temperatures. He even presented a slideshow of his trip. Listening to him, I felt a little stunned. I'd gone to fucking Ireland on my own and hitchhiked around the country without a thought about my leg, never even knowing I might need different socks!

I also attended an ostomy support group meeting. There, I found that unlike myself, most attendees were much older and got their ostomies later in life, due to cancer. At the second meeting, a man talked at length about the "pee bottle" he invented for traveling.

"If you're driving and don't want to stop to take a leak," he said, holding up his invention for all to see, "you can use this."

The man, well meaning, sounded like a huckster. His so-called invention looked no different from the overnight drainage bags I'd used as a child. I had sympathy for the people at the meeting—anyone who could go through what they had gone through had courage, even the guy who invented a travel pee bottle—but listening to so many stories about health problems just made me depressed. After a second meeting, I never went back.

Like my parents, I found this new truth—that it wasn't radiation that caused my birth defects—difficult to comprehend and accept. Having this knowledge, meeting others with the same problems who suffered as I suffered, some of them far worse, and knowing that I wasn't alone in the world, didn't necessarily make me feel less alone. I never blamed my mother, but sometimes I became angry. I discovered that all my life I used "ableist language," when referring to myself and my body. This meant that I allowed others (able-bodied people) to define me. This, I also learned was not uncommon among the disabled.

No matter what the cause or what name you gave my disabilities, it didn't change the fact that I still had to deal with their long-term effects every day. Coming to terms with my body, "accepting the things I could not change," loving myself, and allowing others to love me in return was still a struggle, but the monster in the mirror appeared less and less.

Doomsday

Saturday, September 29, 2012

The day of my death had arrived like a long-awaited prophecy. I was living in an efficiency apartment in Pittsburgh's Highland Park neighborhood. At the time, Leilani and I had been living apart for exactly one month, yet she allowed me to spend the night at her apartment, knowing how scared I was. It would be the last night we spent under the same roof.

Twenty-eight years earlier, when I was thirteen, I'd asked the Ouija board when I would die, and its response was September 29th. It told me I would be 41 years old. When I'd asked how I would die, its answer was more cryptic: M.B.D. This, my mother told me, meant multiple birth defects.

September 29th was like any other day: heavy rains triggered floods in Spain, war raged in Syria, and in Pittsburgh, the Pirates beat the Reds 2-1. Yet, by nightfall I could not bring myself to close my eyes, for fear I wouldn't wake up again. When I finally did give in to sleep, it was dreamless. I woke up the following morning with a sense of relief and renewal, not to mention embarrassment.

How naive and foolish I'd been, to waste twenty-eight years of my life in fear of a date on the calendar, falling under the spell of a parlor game, patented in 1890 by Elijah Jefferson Bond—not a spiritualist with a direct line to the afterlife, but a Confederate soldier from Baltimore, who also had a career as a lawyer. Also: the Ouija board said I would die on a Tuesday, not a Saturday. I decided I never wanted to know what the future had in store.

On the Bus

Thursday, January 17, 2019

All day at work, as patients flowed in and out and the phone kept ringing, I thought about my mother and Jenny at home. Were they getting along? Was my mother taking her medicine? Was she in pain? Should I have called off work to help?

At 4:45 p.m., I was on the bus, heading home. We were stopped in front of the art museum. Traffic, as usual, was backed up for blocks. Even though every seat was taken, and people were standing in the aisle, the bus driver continued to let passengers onboard.

I leaned my head against the window and closed my eyes. When I woke, it felt as if hours had passed. The night before, as I fed my mother orange juice through a straw, she told me that she was proud of me. She said I was a good man. Was I? I had my doubts.

My Mother's Sex Life

Thursday, January 17, 2019

My mother had been living with Jenny and me for just over a week. Her moods and overall condition seemed to fluctuate by the day, sometimes, even by the hour. She spent her days either sleeping or fingering her rosary beads, mumbling her prayers to Jesus, asking Him to end her suffering and take her home. Yet, despite her prayers, she acted as if she wanted to suffer. She'd refused to take any of her medications, including pain relievers, for the past few days. We argued about the medications, but didn't force it.

Now, my mother had grown too weak to make it from the back room to the bathroom, even with her walker and Jenny's help. When she had to go, she ordered me into another room. I was not allowed help with such intimacies, for which I was shamefully relieved. Instead, the job fell to Jenny.

"Let's dance," my mother would say as she clasped her arms around Jenny's neck, and together they made the three or four unsteady steps from the hospital bed, or armchair, to the port-a-potty.

This evening, after "dancing" with Jenny, my mother, back in the gray armchair, nestled under a blanket with her stuffed animals at her side, asked what day it was. When I told her it was Thursday, and that tomorrow Jenny and I were getting married, she asked when Martin Luther King Day was.

"Monday," I said.

"Well," she replied, almost triumphantly. "I'll be dead by then."

Later, with the three of us gathered in the back room, my mother's mood improved. She sat up straight in the armchair. She was talkative. We ordered pizza and she even managed to eat a few bites. We watched an old episode of *Little House on the Prairie*. Then, out of nowhere, my mother asked if we wanted to know about her sex life.

"Yes!" Jenny exclaimed. But I felt confused. I'd never really thought about my mother's sex life before, and the prospects of hearing about it now felt weird, like opening a door to a room that had been forbidden.

My mother asked for a cigarette and lighter. She lit a cigarette, took a deep drag and began her tale. She claimed she'd only had sex twice in her life.

"You only had sex twice," Jenny asked in astonishment, "and one of those times you got pregnant with Jason?"

"I meant with two different men," my mother laughed. "One man, of course, was Jason's father. The other—" She paused, as if deciding if she should go on.

"The other was a guy I was dating," she continued. "We were even going to get married, until I found out he was already married to someone else."

I admit I was shocked to hear my mother had only been with two men in her life. I'd just imagined that when she lived in D.C. she, well... it was the 60s, after all.

"What about Irv?" I blurted out, half joking, but prepared for more surprises. Irv had been her companion for many years.

"Hmph! I don't think so," she said sarcastically, her eyes narrowing in on me, as if she knew I was just trying to get a rise out of her.

Then, she told us about the cross-country road trip she and my father took on their honeymoon. "We drove in your father's

VW," my mother's gravelly voice chimed. As she recounted the adventure, I pictured the two of them posing like Bonnie and Clyde, all sunglasses, large brim hats and goofy, tough-guy grins, and guns—which my father owned. In one of the photos my father stood with his boot on the VW's bumper, looking off into the distance, a gun at his side. In another, my mother—though she never approved of guns—slouched against the side of the car, a pistol in her right hand, pointing at the camera.

As we talked and laughed, I traced the lines on my mother's face with my eyes. At that moment, it seemed impossible to believe that she was dying.

"In Muncie, Indiana," she continued, "Your father posed next to a statue of Paul Bunyan, and I stood next to a statue of a gorilla." They visited The Arch in Saint Louis and the Cowboy Hall of Fame in Oklahoma City. From there, they drove to Tucson.

I found myself trying to calculate the last time my mother might have had sex. My parents separated in 1979 and were divorced two years later. Did they have sex between getting separated and divorced? Had it really been around forty years? As far as I knew, my mother never had a boyfriend after my father. Harry, the TV repairman? Wan, whom I remembered from when my mother worked at U.S. News? Maybe this was a topic sons should not think about regarding their mothers.

"I have only really been in love with two people," my mother finally said, taking another drag off her cigarette. "Your father was not one of them," she said as if for shock value, though I was not shocked. In my mind my parents were worlds apart. But if not my father, then who? My mother's answer: George Grianni and Tom Mroczka.

"George and I went to senior prom together," my mother

said. "He was a great artist. He died of AIDS."

I remember George visiting from the Midwest when I was a teenager. He worked as a graphic designer and claimed he'd gone to college with David Letterman. I knew Tom from City Hall. He was the person who took your money when you paid your water bill. I read his obituary in the newspaper just a day ago but didn't tell my mother.

"Tomorrow's the big day," she winked, and told Jenny how happy she was that we'd found one another. She said we made a great couple. "I never told you before," she said. "But I never liked Leilani."

After a few moments, my mother said she wanted to take a nap. And with that she bent her body sideways, resting her head on the arm of the chair, and closed her eyes.

Wedding Day

Friday, January 18, 2019

I woke up early to pick up the flowers I'd ordered a week ago: a bouquet of white roses and blue hydrangeas for Jenny, and white lilies for my mother. It was hard to believe I was getting married again.

After a volunteer arrived from hospice to stay with my mother, Jenny and I drove to the Wilkinsburg Magistrate's Office where our friends Ben (who was with me the night I met Jenny) and Lauren (Jenny's friend from grad school) were waiting. Jenny wore a blue cardigan over a blue and white lattice-patterned dress, and I wore black pants, an electric blue button-down shirt, and one of my grandfather's ties.

*

Jenny and I met in October 2013 at a poetry reading at Chatham University. The poet Jim Daniels, whom I'd known from Chautauqua, was the headliner. That evening, Jenny introduced Daniels; she was a graduate student, working towards her MFA in poetry and creative nonfiction.

It sounds like a cliché, like a scene from some cheesy movie, but after the reading, as people milled about, I saw Jenny from across the room. With Ben's cajoling, I introduced myself and asked Jenny to join us at a bonfire later that night. In that awkward moment, as bodies hovered around us, voices all talking at once, Jenny politely declined. "I have to go home and bake cookies," she said, and then slipped away into the crowd. Likely story, I thought. Maybe I'd been too presumptuous, too eager. Maybe I was just fooling myself, thinking she'd be interested.

As fate would have it, two weeks later we met again at another poetry reading. Jenny arrived late to the event and I offered her the seat next to mine. That night, I lay awake for hours thinking about her. I couldn't remember her last name, but somehow, I found her—of all places—on Goodreads and sent a message.

Our first date happened on Halloween. We met at Kelly's Tavern, a dark Art Deco bar with blood-red walls and no televisions, and my oasis for the past fourteen months since Leilani and I had separated.

Around five o'clock, Jenny and I claimed two corner stools near the door and talked about literature—Beckett and Basho mostly, politics, travel, and our lives, while pounding down pints of beer and a few shots of whiskey. Before we knew it, three hours had gone by. It felt as if we'd known one another all our lives.

One Sunday morning, a couple of months after our first date, I was standing at the bus stop outside of Jenny's apartment, waiting for the 71B to take me back to my neighborhood, when my mother called.

"Where are you?" she asked. "I hear traffic or wind."

"I'm at the bus stop outside the street from Jenny's apartment."

"Are you sleeping with her?" my mother asked.

For a moment I was stunned by mother's question. We had never talked about sex before. "Yes," I replied, nervously.

"Are you in love?" my mother asked.

"Yes," I said, realizing at that moment that it was true. I'd never felt so in love with anyone in my life.

Like all good things that happened to me, meeting and falling in love with Jenny felt like a fluke, I imagined that once Jenny found out about my ostomies it would be all over. "I'm sorry," she'd say, trying to hide her disgust and shock. "I'm sorry, but I only want to be friends." To my happy surprise, I was wrong. Jenny accepted me with all my scars and deformities.

*

At the Wilkinsburg Magistrate's office, Judge Kim Hoots presided over our wedding ceremony, invoking the name of the Lord more times than I could count. She spoke with spit-fire precision like an auctioneer, pronouncing me and Jenny husband and wife in just three minutes. Afterwards, we went with Ben and Lauren, to The Casbah, an upscale Middle Eastern restaurant, for lunch.

The next day, Jenny and I threw a party to celebrate, inviting all our friends. Somehow, we believed this was a good idea. We thought it might lift my mother's spirits, even take her mind off the fact that she was dying. Even the hospice staff thought it might be a good idea.

We cooked two pots of chili and Jenny's workmates brought a keg of homebrew. Every twenty minutes or so I checked on my mother, bringing her root beer or orange juice. Sometimes I'd even bring friends in to meet her. She smiled and whispered hello, but never once lifted her head from the arm of the chair. Her eyes were big and watery as she stared at us with indifference.

Looking back, I realize how weird it was to introduce my mother to my friends, to have them smile and gawk at her like some sideshow attraction: *Hello, nice to meet you. Sorry to hear that you're dying.* How selfish it was to even think about throwing a party. How could I not see what was so evident—how each day, she grew a little more fragile, each day a little weaker?

A Long Way to Go

Sunday, January 20, 2019

"Today will be my last day on earth," my mother announced. We were losing the battle to get her to take her pain meds. She kept insisting that she wasn't in pain, even though she obviously was. She refused to move from her bed or allow us to reposition her. Anytime we tried, she flinched.

When Tracey arrived, I told her how my mother said that today would be her last day on earth. Tracey said that my mother might be ready to die in her mind, but as far as her body was concerned, she still had a long way to go. She suggested that my mother spend a few days, maybe even a week, at a hospice residency a few miles away, in Munhall. The facility would even permit my mother to smoke if she went outside.

"It would do you all some good," Tracey said. "You all need a break."

It was true, we needed a break, but how could I send my mother away, even for a few days?

My Father Calls

Monday, January 21, 2019

I was sitting in the back room with my mother, watching her drift in and out of sleep, when my cell rang. It was my father. I walked into the dining room, sat at my desk, and answered.

"What's new?" he asked.

"Not much," I replied.

He said he was calling to see how my mother was doing. When I'd first told my father that she had cancer, he replied, "Well, you know what *that's* from, don't you?" as if to say, *What did you expect?* He could talk for hours about other people and their eating habits, about the fact that they drank or smoked too much, about how, unlike him, they didn't take care of themselves.

Now, feeling my anger rise, I wanted to scream. I wanted to say everything I'd been afraid to say my whole life, to stand up for myself and my mother. Instead, I told him how difficult it was getting her to take her pain meds, how she could no longer stand, let alone make it to the bathroom.

What I didn't tell him was that my mother continued to smoke, that since she'd arrived in Pittsburgh, she'd been smoking more than ever. "Like a fiend," as Jenny described it. It was as if she was doing all she could to die as quickly and painfully as possible.

The truth was my father had mellowed some with age. Was it his own fear of death? Or empathy, something I rarely gave him credit for? Either way, he'd been trying to make amends in his own way. He drove me to grad school my second year at

Sarah Lawrence. It was our first and only overnight, out-of-town trip together. Another time he gave me half his winnings when he won $1,000 on the lottery. He attended my graduation, even buying a new suit for the occasion, and when my grandmother died, he brought one of the quilts she'd made and gave it to my mother. The fact that he liked Jenny made me very happy. Still, there was that part of our past we never spoke of. At least for me, it was always there, hanging over our heads, always on the cusp of recognition.

From the back bedroom, as my father talked about some TV show he'd been watching—one of those shows that hadn't had a new episode in over twenty years—my mother called out, "Hang up! Hang up the phone!" Her voice was loud and indignant like a growl.

Could she tell by my mumbled responses, and the long silences in between, that it was my father on the phone?

My parents had been divorced for almost forty years and had only been in one another's company a handful of times since. It had been over two years since they'd last seen each other—at a poetry reading I gave at Chautauqua—and even then, they hardly spoke.

"Hang up!" my mother screamed again, making it clear to all that she had neither forgotten nor forgiven the past.

The Lord's Prayer

Monday, January 21 – Tuesday, January 22, 2019

My mother's mood swings had become erratic. One moment she seemed content listening to music, the next she was depressed, staring with a faraway look in her eyes. She grew disoriented, unsure at times, whether it was night or day, whether she was still alive or had already died.

Monday night, I fell asleep in the gray armchair, as my mother lay in the hospital bed. It was Martin Luther King Day, and despite her prediction that she'd die that day, she had survived. At 2:00 a.m. her restless groans woke me. I asked if she was okay, if she needed anything. She shook her head and stared at me, her eyes watering and big.

"I'm sorry I lost the house," she finally said. "I'm sorry for smoking, for getting cancer."

After a long silence, she asked if I remembered the Lord's Prayer.

"Of course," I replied.

"Will you say it with me?"

While we recited it, I thought of the scene from *Ulysses* when Stephen Dedalus refused to pray with his dying mother. I knew no matter what I believed, I could not refuse my mother's request.

When we finished, my mother told me not to be scared if my grandfather appeared. "He may come to take me to heaven," she said.

Remembering how she claimed to have seen my great-grandfather's ghost right after my grandfather died, I looked in the corners of the room for some sign of his presence. The thought of seeing my grandfather's ghost terrified me.

Have a Good Life

Tuesday, January 22, 2019

Tuesday was another busy day at the urology clinic. During my lunch break, I called my mother. When I asked how she was feeling, she didn't answer, but I could hear her breathing. After a brief silence, she asked when I would be coming home.

"I'm at work," I said. "I'll be home in the evening."

"That's too long. I can't wait," she said. "Take care of yourself. Have a good life."

She sounded like my nana. When I was sixteen, I visited Geraldine and Phil in New Jersey for a week. "I'll be dead by the time you come back," she assured me. My grandfather was also versed in the same guilt trip. He gave me the same bleak warning when, in June 2001, I drove cross-country with a friend.

By keeping me close, did my nana and grandfather believe that not only I, but that they too, would be safe, that nothing bad could happen as long as we were together?

When I came home from work that evening, my mother greeted me with a smile. She never mentioned our phone conversation and I presumed she had no memory of it. I brought her "pulp"—what she now called orange juice. "Pulp!" she chirped like a baby bird. "Bring me pulp!" After she drank her pulp, we sat and talked. When she was tired of talking, we sat in silence. There were still moments to be thankful for.

The Coal Black Sea

Thursday, January 24, 2019

3:00 a.m,. I wake in darkness to find my mother and me adrift on a coal-black sea. I hear the splash of waves, hear the oarsman's raspy breath, and the oar's steady rhythm.

I wake in amniotic silence to find my mother staring at me, her eyes wide and black as portholes.

Am I awake or asleep? Are we here or drifting on a dark sea? I want to ask the oarsman where he's taking us, but somehow, I already know.

"You have to let me go," my mother says, as if she were a kite whose string I greedily clutched in my fist. "Please Jay! Please, do you promise?"

"Yes. Yes, I promise."

Saint Teresa

Thursday, January 24, 2019

On Thursday morning I was at work when Jenny emailed: *All your mom wants is for me to feed her ice chips. She refuses to take the morphine.*

When I think of my mother during those last three or four days at the end of January, refusing to take pain medication, refusing to be comforted, I am reminded of my mother's favorite saint, Saint Teresa of Avila. "Suffering," Teresa wrote, "is a great favor...Blessed is he who came into the world for no other purpose than to suffer."

An hour later, Jenny sent another email: *Any time I mention morphine she gets upset. She begs me not to give it to her. She wants me to cancel the nurse's visit.*

In her autobiography, Saint Teresa describes the ascent of the soul toward God in four stages, or devotions. In the fourth devotion—The Devotion of Ecstasy—she writes: [C]*onsciousness of being in the body disappears. Sensory faculties no longer work. Memory and imagination also become absorbed in God, as though intoxicated. Body and spirit dwell in the throes of exquisite pain.*

In the afternoon, a third email arrived. Jenny and my mother had a heart to heart, and though my mother's spirits were still low, she was slightly better than in the morning. Jenny tidied up the back room and shaved the stray hairs that grew from my mother's chin. She said she felt hopeful about the nurse's visit.

Active Dying

Friday, January 25 – Saturday, January 26, 2019

On Friday morning, my mother's screams woke me. "Get this body out of here!" she demanded. "I died an hour ago."

A couple of hours later, she called out again. Jenny and I ran into the back room to find my mother slowly sliding off the bed feet first. We managed to maneuver her into a more stable position, but she remained contorted and refused to let us move her further. I called Tracey, who said she'd be over soon. Then, I called off work.

My mother allowed Tracey to reposition her so that her head rested on the pillow at the top of the bed. She also reluctantly accepted a dose of morphine. "It only hurts when I move," she said. When the morphine started to take effect, Tracey motioned for Jenny and me to follow her into the living room.

"Your mother's legs and toes are mottled," she whispered. "They're cold to the touch," Tracey told us that these were signs that my mother was now in what hospice called the active dying stage—the final stage.

"It's like she took a drastic turn overnight," I said.

"She's not been the same since the party, really," Jenny admitted.

On Facebook I received a message from Amanda, who lived an hour north of Pittsburgh, in Meadville. She asked if Saturday would be a good day to visit.

It's been a bad day, I typed in reply. But I urged Amanda to come if she could. My mother would be happy to see her.

Later that evening, my mother was feeling better. She, Jenny, and I watched *The Guernsey Literary and Potato Peel Pie Society*, a film about a book club in the Channel Islands during World War Two. My mother watched with interest but fell asleep before the film ended. When she woke up, she asked what had happened. She wanted to know if Juliet and Dawsey got together. Even then—her breathing shallow, her skin mottled—her mind was still curious, still engaged in the world around her.

*

Amanda arrived around one o'clock on Saturday, with a bouquet of painted daisies for my mother. We stood around the bed and talked with my mother until she fell asleep. Then, Amanda, Jenny, and I went into the kitchen where we sat around the table. It all felt surreal, yet strangely normal: the three of us eating pizza, telling stories of our youth, laughing, then crying, while just two rooms away, my mother lay dying.

Nineteen Days

Sunday, January 27, 2019

In the middle of the night my mother woke up screaming again. This time Jenny and I found her frantically grabbing at the blankets and sheets. "My cigarette," she yelled. "I dropped my cigarette!"

We looked through the tangle of sheets, but found no cigarette. After my mother calmed, Jenny and I assured her that she'd just been dreaming (though I'm not sure she really believed us), and we returned to bed.

When we woke up again, around 8:00 a.m., my mother had lost the ability to speak. Her lips moved, but there was no sound. Did she have a stroke? Had the cancer wormed its way into her cerebrum? Tracey arrived, hooked my mother up to the supplemental oxygen machine we had stored in a closet, and told us to watch for signs of agitation. "The active dying stage," she said, "could last several days."

Throughout the afternoon, I kept vigil at my mother's bedside, holding her hand and rubbing ice chips on her lips. I told her how much I loved her, and how grateful I was for all she'd done for me. On YouTube, Dean Martin sang "On the Street Where You Live" as I counted her labored breaths—deep gasps every 3 ½ seconds, her unflinching, cloudy gaze fixed upon some distant point.

Around quarter to four, I decided to take a shower. Despite her shallow breathing, my mother seemed stable. Jenny suggested we recite the rosary. "We can say it after your shower," she said. "Maybe it will be comforting for your mom."

While I was in the bathroom, I heard Jenny's voice. She was speaking into our new, voice-activated remote control, part of the cable package we'd bought for my mother. "*The Waltons*," I heard Jenny shout. "Play *The Waltons*."

A few minutes later, Jenny was calling my name, asking me to come out of the bathroom. When I walked into the bedroom, Jenny stood staring at my mother.

"I was trying to find *The Waltons*," she said. "When I turned back around, she wasn't breathing."

I approached her bed and began shouting "Mom! Mom!" like I'd done as a child, on those school mornings when her alarm clock woke me, and I hobbled into her bedroom begging her to wake up. Now, like then, she did not respond.

She looked so small, like a toy version of herself, like a figurine carved from wood. Her eyes were still open, her mouth ajar, with an expression of astonishment. What, or who had she seen? In her last moments, did my mother's own life pass before her? Had my grandfather come, like she thought he might? Her grandmother? Aunt Rose? Saint Teresa? Had a ring of angels come to bear her up on eagle's wings? Or was she still adrift on a coal-black sea?

"What will it take to break you?" she asked a few days earlier. I refused to let her see me cry. I refused to break down. Now, holding her lifeless hand in mine, I sobbed. I felt like I'd felt that night in the emergency room, when the doctor told my mother that she had cancer, like I'd fallen through a trap door.

It had only been nineteen days since my mother moved to Pittsburgh. The truth was, I was still a child. Never having children of my own, I'd never experienced that sense of responsibility, that desperate need to protect another person, that parents feel. I never sacrificed for anyone like my mother sacrificed for me. Suddenly, I understood what my mother needed, what she craved all her life: to be mothered, to be cherished, and loved tenderly the way she had loved me. Unable to admit that she was dying, I foolishly spent the last few weeks arguing with her about taking her medications. I knew, because of this, that I failed her in some elemental way.

My mother's death was not one of those dramatic deaths you see in the movies. There were no revelations brought to light, no final words. Instead, her death happened quietly, almost unnoticed, like driving through some tiny town with only one traffic light. She just slipped away, leaving behind the shell of her body, like a chrysalis.

Epilogue: Everything's Alright

2019

As a child, I used to imagine my death would be dramatic, and in the afterlife, my ghost would float just off the periphery, watching the living as if through a two-way mirror. Yet, it is impossible to truly comprehend our own deaths, to fathom that one day we will no longer exist and our loved ones who survive us will move on, and experience joys and sorrows without us. Even when those we love die, we somehow hold on to the idea of our own immortality. How could we live otherwise?

And like every generation that's come before, we believe that our lives—our aspirations and dreams, the times in which we live—are most important. If we're lucky, some small memory of us will live on for a time—a laugh, a turn of phrase, an act of kindness we performed, or words written down on sheets of paper. But in the end, we too will be forgotten.

The day her obituary appeared in the *Evening Observer*, Jenny and I drove to Dunkirk to clean out her apartment. On our arrival we were greeted by an old-fashioned winter storm. High winds blew off the lake and the temperature hovered around three degrees.

In a trunk in my mother's bedroom, I found a doll with button eyes, my mother's baptismal dress, and a cross made from palms given to her by her aunt Rose. There were dozens of drawings and cards I'd made for her, poems and stories I'd written, awards I'd won, as well as a speeding ticket from 1991. In a manila envelope, under rosary beads and miscellaneous funeral cards, I found the brown, rubber feeding tube that nourished me during the first year of my life.

If there was a moment that week that made Jenny and me laugh, something that lessened the stress and sadness we felt, it came when we opened a large FedEx envelope filled with smaller envelopes, all holding tiny bottles of CBD oil. After her stroke, my mother started reading about the curative wonders of CBD. I bought her a bottle of CBD cream from a pharmacy in Pittsburgh, but not before she ordered a "free sample" from an ad she'd seen on the internet.

"It was on CNN," she'd insisted. "It comes from Cornell University. So, it must be legit."

I knew she'd received a few samples, but even when she told me the free samples kept arriving, I didn't understand that she meant every month. She used my aunt Stephanie's credit card to pay, supposedly for shipping. My aunt would later admit she'd paid hundreds of dollars.

Along with the CBD oils was a box of essential oils—eucalyptus, peppermint, hyssop, and lavender—a gift from my mother's friend Jackie. The oils came with a diffuser, which turned the oil into steam. They were supposed to boost energy and relieve stress. Maybe my mother hoped the oils would somehow cure her cancer, or at least stop it from spreading.

At the bottom of the trunk lay the flower-shaped music box that used to hang on my nana's kitchen door, the one that Aiesha and I played over and over, the one that my nana used to torment my mother and uncle with. Had my mother kept it all these years as a reminder? Was it a form of penance? I pulled the greasy string one last time and listened to the eerie tune. Then I handed it to Jenny, who hurled it forcefully down the garbage chute.

In my mother's closet, we found clothes she hadn't worn

in years, including a winter coat that I'd bought her several Christmases ago, a plaid button-down with wide collars. For decades, my mother only shopped at Goodwill or the Salvation Army, rarely treating herself to such extravagances as new clothes. She made trips to thrift stores an adventure, a place where you could find treasures, not a place where you shopped because you had no money.

Jenny and I donated my mother's clothes, kitchenware, and furniture to the Rural Ministry (part of the soup kitchen where I used to volunteer). We divided up her books and records, and donated the ones we didn't want, or didn't have room for, to the local Literacy Volunteers bookstore and the Salvation Army.

By the end of the week, my mother's apartment was empty of any trace of her. I took a last walk through. Soon someone else's mother, father, aunt, or uncle would be moving in. Suddenly, I felt like an orphan, like I no longer belonged here—in this town, anywhere. But of course, I had Jenny. I also had my aunt and uncle, my cousins, my friends, and even my father.

*

One morning, nine months after my mother's death, while I stood waiting for the bus to take me to work, I listened to her voicemails that I'd saved on my cell phone.

Hi Jay, one message began. *It's just me. I wonder if you could, on your way home, stop at the drive-thru at CVS and pick up my meds?*

In another message from November of 2018, she says: *It's about quarter to eight, just wondering how far away you are. I hope the weather's alright for youse. Alright, bye.*

I still find it difficult to comprehend that my mother is

really gone, that she'll never again open her apartment door and greet me with her wide smile. Sometimes I imagine I'll see her ghost lurking in the corners, that I'll feel her presence, but I haven't yet.

I've become obsessed with the thought of my own death. Some nights I wake, gripped by a sense of bewilderment, and fear—the timebomb in my chest pounding, my mother's voice somewhere far off, calling: *See, I told you so. Whatever.*

Other nights, when I can't sleep, I sit at my desk under the glow of a lamp and, with pencil and ruler in hand, I draw the floorplans to the house on Main Street like a mad cartographer, as if by doing so, I can somehow return to those rooms, to that safety.

"These fragments," T.S. Eliot writes toward the end of *The Waste Land*, "I have shored against my ruins." Isn't that what I was doing now, what I've done my entire life—gathering fragments of memories like shards of glass, or the photographs Aiesha and I found at my grandparents' house—as if they could protect me and stave off my own inevitable ruin?

In *Mourning Diary,* a diary begun after the death of his mother, in October 1975, French literary theorist, philosopher, and critic Roland Barthes writes, "[T]hat this death fails to destroy me altogether means that I want to live wildly, madly, and that therefore the fear of my own death is always there, not displaced by a single inch."

In another entry, Barthes ponders whether being able to live without his mother means he loves her less than he once thought. "In my mind I still see my mother sitting there on the hospital bed, eyes wide open, dead." He writes about how the image of his mother during the months of her dying had become fuzzy. He fears, as I fear, that in another year, the image of her face, her voice, her laughter, will grow so cloudy that he'll no longer be able to conjure it or the emotions it once stirred in him.

I know that none of my successes could have been possible without my mother's constant love and encouragement. She was the only person who saw me as the person I dreamed of being. If not for her, I may well have been put in an institution like Sister Maurine had suggested nearly fifty years ago. Maybe the reason I survived all those hospitalizations and surgeries was not because I was destined for greatness, but to be with my mother when she left this world.

If she were alive today, she'd no doubt shake her head and chuckle at my lack of self-confidence, my impatience, my sparks of anger.

"Relax," she'd say. "Be thankful. Be happy. Everything's alright," and I'd have no choice but to believe her.

Acknowledgments

Thanks to all those who've read early drafts and encouraged me to keep going: Gerry Crinnin, Scott Jardin, Kristin Kovacic, Kevin Pilkington, Dawn Raffel and Lauren Turner, as well as Pam Kirst, Scott Silsbe, Dan Jackson, Eric Zwieg and Tracy Astwood, for the time and effort they put into helping me turn this manuscript into a book. Big thank yous to Jan Beatty, Ed Simon, Tim Parrish, and Wioletta Grzegorzewska. Thank you to Kevin Atticks and eveyone at Apprentice House.

I also want to thank Kris Collins (*Pittsburgh Book Review*) and Michael Simms (*Vox Populi*), as well as the editors of the following journals where excerpts and chapters, in various forms and versions have appeared: *Lenticular*, *Panorama*, *Rust Belt Press*, *Santa Ana Review*, *A Thin Slice of Anxiety*, *Toasted Cheese*, and *Wordgathering*.

Most of all, thank you to Jen Ashburn for sharing her life with me, for her love and belief in me, for putting up with my endless self-doubts and weirdness, and finally my mother.

About the Author

Jason Irwin is the author of three books of poetry: *The History of Our Vagrancies* (Main Street Rag, 2020), *A Blister of Stars* (Low Ghost, 2016) and *Watering the Dead*, winner of the Transcontinental Poetry Award (Pavement Saw Press, 2008). He lives in Pittsburgh with his wife, writer, Jen Ashburn.

Apprentice House is the country's only campus-based, student-staffed book publishing company. Directed by professors and industry professionals, it is a nonprofit activity of the Communication & Media Department at Loyola University Maryland.

Using state-of-the-art technology and an experiential learning model of education, Apprentice House publishes books in untraditional ways. This dual responsibility as publishers and educators creates an unprecedented collaborative environment among faculty and students, while teaching tomorrow's editors, designers, and marketers.

Eclectic and provocative, Apprentice House titles intend to entertain as well as spark dialogue on a variety of topics. Financial contributions to sustain the press's work are welcomed. Contributions are tax deductible to the fullest extent allowed by the IRS.

To learn more about Apprentice House books or to obtain submission guidelines, please visit www.apprenticehouse.com.

Apprentice House Press
Communication & Media Department
Loyola University Maryland
4501 N. Charles Street
Baltimore, MD 21210
Ph: 410-617-5265
info@apprenticehouse.com • www.apprenticehouse.com

www.ingramcontent.com/pod-product-compliance
Lightning Source LLC
LaVergne TN
LVHW010607100826
845148LV00014B/2880

* 9 7 8 1 6 2 7 2 0 6 3 9 6 *